A PLACE FO

A PLACE FOR GOD

GRAHAM JAMES

BLOOMSBURY

LONDON · OXFORD · NEW YORK · NEW DELHI · SYDNEY

Bloomsbury Continuum
An imprint of Bloomsbury Publishing Plc

50 Bedford Square
London
WC1B 3DP
UK

1385 Broadway
New York
NY 10018
USA

www.bloomsbury.com

BLOOMSBURY, CONTINUUM and the Diana logo are trademarks of
Bloomsbury Publishing Plc

First published 2017

British Library Cataloguing-in-Publication Data
A catalogue record for this book is available from the British Library.

Library of Congress Cataloguing-in-Publication data has been applied for.

ISBN:
PB: 9781472945266
ePDF: 9781472945242
ePub: 9781472945259

2 4 6 8 10 9 7 5 3 1

Typeset by Newgen KnowledgeWorks Pvt. Ltd., Chennai, India
Printed and bound in Great Britain by CPI Group (UK) Ltd, Croydon CR0 4YY

To find out more about our authors and books visit www.bloomsbury.com.
Here you will find extracts, author interviews, details of forthcoming events
and the option to sign up for our newsletters.

CONTENTS

Contents

INTRODUCTION

Whenever I am asked, 'Where do you come from?' I refer invariably to my Cornish ancestry. Yet I have spent only 16 years of my life in my native county. Origins and identity matter to me, as they do to most people. We want to place ourselves in the world. I was tempted to call this book 'Location, location, vocation' because my sense of vocation, both as a Christian and as a priest, has been related more to place than I have sometimes been willing to admit.

Like many clergy I have encountered a deep loyalty to place, which can lead to a parochial outlook that is unwilling to see value in being linked with that parish next door and hesitant about any form of change. Loyalty to place is not always liberating, and yet it is unmistakeable that location matters in the Christian story. Jerusalem, Bethlehem, Nazareth, Capernaum: the places we associate with Jesus are real enough for millions of people today. Whenever I lead a pilgrimage to the Holy Land, I am reminded how frequently locations are identified by name in the Gospels. The Christian faith is not a philosophical abstraction.

All places of encounter with the divine become holy to us. They may not be regarded as sacred by others but there is no limitation on where we may meet God, encounter Jesus Christ or receive a gift of the Holy Spirit. There was nothing originally sacred about the place we know as Bethel. But it became a holy place when Abram built an altar there on his way to Egypt (Genesis 12) and its sacred character was assured when Jacob dreamt there of a ladder stretching from heaven to earth (Genesis 28). Jacob anointed the stone he used as a pillow. The name of Bethel ('house of God') became, centuries later, a common designation for nonconformist chapels in England and Wales. Even a tradition with a very limited understanding of sacred space (and some-times hostility to the very idea) found that Bethel, and other biblical names such as Moriah, Ebenezer and Bethesda, were acceptable dedications for their chapels as places of encounter with the living (and biblical) God.

My earliest years in Cornish nonconformity pro-vided little sense of sacred space beyond the chapels I knew best (two of which are included in a chapter here). I knew them as special places which people dusted and polished, and where they arranged flow-ers, established children's corners, sang hymns, said prayers and engaged in a short but very special service after the main one where small cubes of bread and tiny glasses of wine were distributed. (Children were generally excluded from this additional service, which seemed to be only for the very devout.) Above all, these chapels were not accessible shrines. Outside service times, they were resolutely locked.

When, at the age of 11, I began attending Anglican services (not of my own volition but because of a major change in family allegiance), I sensed an immediate difference. The church we attended was a place of daily worship. It was open for people to pray there whenever they wished. A candle flickered before the Blessed Sacrament. A sense of the presence of God, while mysterious and elusive, was much more definitely located. I became aware that sacred space had a character and identity.

It was much later that my understanding of sacred place and space broadened further, but was challenged too. When Jesus encounters the Samaritan woman at the well, he tells her that in future 'neither on this mountain [Gerizim], nor in Jerusalem, will you worship the Father' (John 4.21). This could be interpreted as the clearest command from the Lord himself that the gospel knows of no special sacred places, no hallowed locations, no pilgrimage beyond our journey through this life. There is

3

only the heavenly Jerusalem to which we are called. Meanwhile, we walk as 'strangers and pilgrims on earth' (1 Peter 2.11). We are called to be living stones in a church without physical construction, which is a sign of God's coming and universal kingdom.

'The earth is the Lord's, and all that is in it …' (Psalm 24.1). That conviction is central to the Hebrew Bible, but there is a discernible tension between God's presence everywhere and the place of his dwelling on earth. The Ark of the Covenant was the manifestation of God's physical presence in this world. When the Ark travelled, it was constantly accompanied by clouds, a common symbol of God's presence. When the High Priest entered the sanctuary on the Day of Atonement, he did so under the cover of a cloud of incense, perhaps to prevent anyone from seeing God in all his glory (Leviticus 16.13).

And yet here we encounter a strange phenomenon in the Hebrew Bible. The holiness of the Ark of the Covenant is so great and so concentrated, so saturated with divinity, that it's dangerous. When the Philistines capture the Ark, some who merely look at it are killed by its power. In Numbers 4.20 we are told that if those who serve the Tabernacle view the Ark at an improper time they will face immediate death.

This is a warning that God is not to be taken lightly, nor is the divine presence a comfortable one. Even Solomon, upon the completion of what may be the greatest religious building the world has ever known, the temple in Jerusalem, exclaims, 'The heaven of heavens cannot contain you. How much less this house that I have built!' (1 Kings 8.27).

This collection of places where I have encountered God in my life does include religious buildings; considering how much time I have spent within them, it would be surprising if it were otherwise. Even so, many of the settings for an encounter with the divine are not conventionally religious, and the experience was not always immediate. Neither was every encounter initially pleasurable, peaceful or joyful. Places and experiences linger in the memory. A perspective subtly changes; a conviction is reshaped; a sense of calling is confirmed; a glimpse of divine joy comes unbeckoned; a sorrow is redeemed.

Occasionally there is fear. The fear of the Lord may be the beginning of wisdom, but if the living God does not sometimes shame us by the purity of holiness and love then we would hear no

call to righteousness and justice at all. Although
there are 40 chapters – one for each day of Lent
for those who wish to read regularly then – this is a
book for every season of the Church's year. It isn't
conventionally devotional, though there is a suggested (and short) reading from scripture related
to each place. A brief prayer concludes each chapter, with two exceptions where the poems quoted
are prayers in themselves. The reflections are far
from exhaustive, but my hope is that enough will
be triggered in the reader's own heart, mind and
experience to aid further contemplation, prayer
and thought. What's written is an invitation to
travel, but the destination is not the sort found
in travel brochures; rather, it is in our pilgrimage
with and to God revealed in Jesus Christ. Our
response to the sort of experiences recorded here
is always fitful and incomplete, but I find it hard to
understand how so many people can live, as they
seem to do, without a place for God.

1

8115 Vila Kazi Street, Orlando West, Soweto, South Africa

Matthew 12.46–50

Nelson Mandela moved to this address with his first wife Evelyn and their eldest son in 1946. It was a standard house built by tender and commissioned by the Johannesburg City authorities. The South West township of Soweto some 15 kilometres from the city centre was then being developed as a place for black South Africans to live. Nelson Mandela said of 8115 Vila Kazi Street, 'It was the opposite of grand, but it was the first true home of my own and I was mightily proud. A man is not a man until he has a house of his own.'

Nelson and Evelyn Mandela divorced in 1957. She had become a Jehovah's Witness and their perspectives on the world diverged significantly. In 1958 he was joined in the house by his second wife, Winnie. He and Winnie scarcely lived a normal married life at all as Mandela became increasingly committed to his campaign for a truly democratic society marked by racial equality and justice. He was absent at the time of the birth of both his daughters. It was not that he was careless of family life, but the vocation which claimed him scarcely permitted it. We can have more than one vocation and they can clash. In 1961 Mandela went underground. Arrested in 1962, he was given a sentence of life imprisonment for treason in 1964.

On his release from prison in 1990, Mandela insisted on returning to the home he had not seen for 30 years. His familiarity with confined space would have meant this small single-storey house might not have seemed too cramped at the time: it was a symbol of the freedom for which he had waited so long. Mandela wrote, 'That night I returned with Winnie to number 8115 … I knew in my heart I had left prison. For me number 8115 was the centre point of my world, the place marked with an X in my mental geography.' A huge crowd gathered outside and when he addressed them Mandela said, 'I have come home at last.'

In the event, Nelson Mandela stayed there for just 11 days. The world's media were camped around this small unprotected property. That, in itself, made any attempt at an ordinary life impossible. It quickly became clear, too, that Nelson and Winnie's marriage, which had never been a lived reality, was not likely to be the supportive context for the life for which Mandela himself yearned. It took him the better part of two years to admit this truth. For his dream of freedom while in prison was linked not just to his house and home but to his family and marriage. The house was a reality. The marriage was not.

Today the house is a museum, the rooms containing original furnishings and Mandela memorabilia. It bears the scars of its history. Scorch marks by the front door are evidence of Molotov cocktails hurled in anger. Bullet holes in the walls betray how this house continued to be a battleground long after Nelson Mandela was imprisoned. Winnie Mandela's prominence in the insurgences against apartheid led to her banishment in 1977. She and her younger daughter were relocated to Brandfordt, a small Afrikaans speaking town in the Free State where scarcely anyone spoke Winnie's native language, Xhosa. The house they were given had no electricity or running water. Winnie remained there under house arrest until 1986. The experience nurtured the belligerent and unpredictable radicalism for which she became noted in later years.

I had known what Nelson Mandela had said about his house well before first visiting 8115 myself.

Its small scale and primitive design were a striking reminder that the freedom of home has little to do with spatial dimensions, facilities and comforts. Within our homes we determine how we will live. Our sense of freedom is also related to our ability to come and go from home as we please. Those were precisely the freedoms which Mandela, like other prisoners, was denied for so long. No wonder home and freedom are so interlinked in the human imagination.

Even so, Mandela could not stay there if he was to fulfil his mission following his release. It would have become another prison. Although Jesus seems to have lived at home in Nazareth for most of his earthly life, his mission could not be completed from there either. He had to leave home to call disciples, preach and teach, suffer and die. When he began his ministry, his mother and the rest of his family sought him out to ask him to come home. After all, he had no need to rely on the hospitality of others; he had a family who would care for him. What did Mary make of being told by her son as he looked around at those with whom he was talking, 'Here are my mother and my brothers. For whoever does the will of my father in heaven is my brother and sister and mother' (Matthew 12.49, 50)? But this was part of bringing a wider family into being, one in which the relationships are intimate but where ties of blood matter less than ties of common faith.

When Nelson Mandela died, Rowan Williams said of him, 'Most politicians represent an interest group, a community of people who vote for them and whose interests they serve. Nelson Mandela was different; he represented a community that did not yet exist, a community he hoped would come into being.'

When he proclaimed the coming kingdom of God, Jesus spoke of a community that did not yet exist. A sign of that coming kingdom is found in the Church. The relationships between the members of the body of Christ reveal, and sadly sometimes obscure, that sign. Jesus speaks of a home beyond any earthly home, one where we find the fullest freedom and the greatest liberation. Redefining home does not diminish our love of our earthly homes but enlarges our understanding of where God intends our home to be.

Bless, Lord, our homes with your presence and protection, and give us the courage to follow you when you lead us to fresh ventures and to unknown places. Amen.

2

Pool St Martin's, Cornwall

Hebrews 6.10–12

Next door to my grandmother's house at Pool, situated midway between Redruth and Camborne in Cornwall, there was a Methodist chapel. That part of Cornwall was once super-endowed with Methodist chapels. But this one had a surprising dedication. It was called Pool St Martin's. None of my family went there, despite living so near. Their Methodist chapel (a Wesleyan one) was 200 yards away. It was built in 1862, precisely the same year as Pool St Martin's, a testimony to both the vigour and division of Methodism in the Victorian age.

When I was in training for ordination in the Church of England in the early 1970s, I had a conversation with a local Methodist in Pool. I remarked that it was unusual for a Cornish Methodist chapel to be dedicated to someone like St Martin of Tours. It had been originally built as

a United Methodist Free Church and so origin-
ated from that part of Methodism with a rugged
independent streak. What inspired its founders to
dedicate this chapel to a French bishop from the
fourth century?

As it turned out, St Martin of Tours had nothing
to do with it. 'That chapel was named after Martin
Andrew. He went there every Sunday for fifty years.
Everyone thought he was a saint. We renamed the
chapel after him when he died.'

It is the only example I know of Cornish Methodists
making someone a saint by acclamation. There
was no canonization process. They were being
ruggedly independent. They knew a saint of God
when they saw one. They had no need to ask the
central authorities of their denomination for permission. I do not expect they realized they were
doing what Catholic Christians a millennium or
more earlier would have done, both in Cornwall
and other Celtic lands where the names of saints
survive in place names even when we know nothing else about them.

It is a glorious tradition to name a church or a community after those whose spiritual lives were so transparent to God that others saw God in and through

them. The major difference, of course, between the
Cornish Methodists at Pool St Martin's and those
in earlier centuries who made saints by acclamation
is that in earlier times a local cult of the saint often
developed. I doubt that Martin Andrew was ever
invoked in the prayers at Pool St Martin's. I'm sure
his intercession was not sought as one who was near
the throne of grace (though they would have believed
he was). Candles were not lit before a statue of him,
no relics preserved and no shrine sustained his memory beyond the generation of those who knew him.

In 1976 when Pool St Martin's closed, Martin
Andrew's name was lost with the building. For the
past 40 years it has been the Dreadnought Centre,
doing valuable work among children and young
people with emotional, physical or behavioural dif-
ficulties. When the centre was established in 1978,
I wonder if anyone knew the history of the naming
of the chapel. St Martin of Tours was famous for
cutting his cloak in half to clothe a naked beggar
at Amiens. There are stories of St Martin healing
lepers or those mentally distressed and reaching
out to the marginalized. Strangely, the compassionate work that has been done in the old Pool
St Martin's has been entirely in keeping with the
much more famous St Martin of Tours. This may
be God working in his usual mysterious way.

In 1862, when two Methodist chapels were built in Pool within a stone's throw of each other, Wesleyan Methodists and United Free Methodists had very little mutual love. Pool Wesley was much the bigger chapel. It was where my parents were married. It closed in 2012 but, somewhat ironically, it has now become the home of a Free Methodist congregation, entirely independent of the mainstream Methodist Church. The spirit of Pool St Martin's lives on in its ex-Wesleyan neighbour.

As a young priest in only my second post, I returned to my parents' chapel to speak at a mid-week fellowship meeting. Three of the local preachers who had begun their ministries in Pool Wesley just before the Second World War had gone on to become Anglican priests. That Methodist chapel was a better vocation factory for the Church of England than the vast majority of Anglican churches. They did not seem in the least resentful but were rather proud of this unlikely fact. Our fellowship meeting took place in what was known as 'No. 3 Vestry'. One man there recalled his conversion in that very room many years earlier. He said, 'No. 3 Vestry here at Pool Wesley is the most sacred place on earth for me.' 'My Bethel,' he called it, recalling Genesis 28 where Jacob dreams of a ladder connecting earth and heaven with angels ascending and descending.

No. 3 Vestry was devoid of architectural interest or devotional aids. It was a very bare room. But it was a sacred place. Jacob said of the equally unprepossessing place he called Bethel, 'This is none other than the House of God, this is the Gate of Heaven.' In Hebrew, as noted in the Introduction, 'Bethel' means 'House of God'.

I discovered from Nicholas Holtam, currently Bishop of Salisbury and previously Vicar of St Martin-in-the-Fields, that when that church was consecrated in October 1726 the vicar preached about Jacob's dream at Bethel, focusing particularly upon the angels. There are at least 70 angels painted on to the ceiling of that great London church as a vivid reminder that a house of God is intended to be the gate of heaven too. My early formation was spent in a nonconformist tradition which eschewed images, sacred places, invocation of saints and shrines. Yet it also revealed the way Christians honour holiness in individual lives, cherish the memory of those the Church usually calls saints, and revere even the plainest places where God is encountered. As I look back, these things have helped form my later Christian life more than I may have ever anticipated.

God of heaven, you make your home on earth
and sanctify even the plainest places with your

presence. Help us to treasure the locations
where we find you and the lives of those
you have touched with the fullness of your
grace. Amen.

3

The Pantheon, Rome

Matthew 5.14–16

When Michelangelo saw the Pantheon in Rome for the first time he is reported to have said that it looked more like the work of angels than of human beings. In November 1979 I was captivated by the Pantheon's beauty and proportions on the drabbest and wettest of winter days. Unlike so many of the ruined buildings of ancient Rome, here was one in continuous use since its construction in AD 125. Even to my untrained eye, the Pantheon's proportions seemed perfect. So they are. The diameter of the dome, 142 feet, is the exact equivalent of its height from the ground to the centre of the dome. The hole at the top (the oculus) is the only source of light for the whole building. Even on my first visit I noticed that it seemed to rain more lightly inside than out. There is an almost invisible drainage system in the floor, with tiny holes that prevent the water from settling in any quantity. Even now, the exact composition of the material used to build the dome is open to debate. It seems very similar to modern concrete though with much longer-lasting properties.

At the Pantheon the sophistication of ancient Rome is visible for all to see. Even so, its original purpose still has elements of obscurity. Its name suggests it was built to honour all the gods. The statues of the gods – Jupiter, Mars, Venus, Juno, Minerva, Bacchus etc. – were found in the niches of its walls. Whether it was a temple where sacrifices were offered is unknown. It has been suggested that the rising smoke and incense of sacrifices would have escaped through the oculus. This seems unlikely. There was no cult of all the gods. We don't know what, if any, pagan worship went on in the Pantheon. There are times, though, when the sun shines through the oculus and can illuminate a figure standing in the portico. So if the Roman Emperor stood there, it could be that this building would have demonstrated his divinity as part of a great constellation of gods. The Pantheon may simply have been built to impress. It does, even to this day.

The Pantheon became a Christian church consecrated to St Mary and the Martyrs on 13 May 609, a gift of the Byzantine Emperor Phocas. This building constructed to honour pagan gods became a place where Jesus Christ was worshipped, and where our Lord's mother and all the martyrs were commemorated. 'All Saints' Day', as it became known, was celebrated on 13 May for about a century until Pope Gregory III moved it to 1 November, on which day the feast has been observed in the universal Church ever since.

My later visits to the Pantheon have often been in bright sunshine. I have observed that many of my fellow visitors did not look up to the oculus until it was pointed out to them. The light floods from this into the Pantheon. There is much of interest for it to illuminate. We don't often look to the source of light itself – indeed, to look at the sun can be dangerous – but we rely on light to see the world as it is. In the Sermon on the Mount, Jesus says to his followers, 'You are the light of the world.' He speaks about putting a light on the lampstand so that it illuminates all the house, before going on to say, 'Let your light shine before others, so that they may see your good works and give glory to your Father in heaven' (Matthew 5.16). That text is one of those I heard most frequently in my formative years when the Book of Common Prayer formed my main liturgical diet. At the Parish Eucharist each week that sentence was said before the offertory. There are no fewer than 20 possible texts to choose from in the Prayer Book communion service but, being the first, this one was invariably used. Perhaps the sudden range of choice, unusual in the Book of Common Prayer, was more than most celebrants welcomed.

That text always seemed to me to be plain contrary to instructions Jesus gives in Matthew 23, where the Pharisees are criticized for doing 'all their deeds to be seen by others'. If we are not to let our right hand know what our left hand is doing, how are we consciously to display our good works? It took time for me to recognize that what Jesus asks of us is to be light to others, and light always gives itself away. Our good works are always given away – an offering. They are not to draw attention to our virtue (which may anyway be in limited supply).

Perhaps this is why, curiously, the Feast of All Saints has its origin in a church dedicated to 'St Mary and the Martyrs'. On All Saints' Day we think of Christians in every generation who are not formally canonized but who have illuminated the lives of others by their faith, service and example. But the martyrs? Why were they given such prominence in the dedication of this church from which emanated the universal celebration of All Saints' Day?

Michael Stancliffe, sometime Dean of Winchester, once preached an All Saints' sermon recalling the way in which the Emperor Nero blamed any public disturbance on Christians. Tacitus tells us that Christians were dipped in tar when still alive and tied to trees and poles and set alight. Tacitus had little regard for the Christian faith but even in a culture where public entertainment frequently involved human cruelty, this sort of treatment of a despised minority was sickening.

These Christians may not have been conspicuously virtuous, mission-minded or theologically articulate, but they were faithful to death. They let their light shine before others. Whether it was St Lawrence on his gridiron or St Catherine on her wheel, there is a long tradition of martyrs illuminating not just the place of their execution but the life of the Church down the ages. They gave away both light and their lives. The Pantheon oculus, channelling its light into the church below, has existed for almost the entire Christian era. It is a good place to give thanks for all the saints, but perhaps especially for the martyrs whose light still shines and gives glory to our Father in heaven.

*Bring your light, Lord, to the dark places of
our world through those whose lives burn with
your sacrificial love and who give glory to
you. Amen.*

4

Shepherds' Fields, Beit Sahour

Luke 2.8–12

There are no fewer than three locations near Bethlehem that claim to be the place where the shepherds were visited by a heavenly host of angels on the first Christmas night. One is the reputed site of the Tower of Eder, where Jacob was said to have settled after his wife Rachel died (Genesis 35.21). The early Church historian Eusebius claimed that the tower, reckoned to be a thousand paces from Bethlehem, also marked the place where the shepherds received the angels' message. It's the site favoured by the Orthodox.

Another less well-attested site with some large caves is home to a YMCA centre. This is referred to as 'the Protestant' Shepherds' Fields. Since shepherds used caves for shelter in biblical times, it is perhaps the easiest place in which to imagine the scene of the biblical story.

The most visited of the sites is in the keeping of the Franciscan Custody of the Holy Land and located just outside Beit Sahour. It also contains a cave that makes an atmospheric underground place of worship, as well as various outdoor altars and a modern Chapel of the Angels designed by the Italian architect Antonio Barluzzi. The chapel is shaped to look like a tent and possesses marvellous acoustics. It has three wall paintings, telling the story of the angels coming to the shepherds, the visit to the manger, and the shepherds' return to the fields.

The elevated position and spaciousness of this site at Beit Sahour mean that pilgrims and visitors are frequently more moved than they expect. The better one gets to know it, however, the more appropriately disturbing it becomes. The place where it is believed the birth of the Prince of Peace was announced is a place where there is no peace.

The panorama from the Shepherds' Fields is one in which the separation wall in the West Bank snakes its way through the valley below. Large Israeli settlements cling to the hillside and claim significant amounts of land in the Bethlehem Governorate. The visible evidence of a divided society is laid out before your eyes.

The Israelis regard the separation wall as a security barrier against terrorism. It has undoubtedly reduced random attacks. Israeli support for the wall seems strong and enduring. Around Bethlehem the wall is eight metres high, almost twice the height of the former Berlin Wall. Separation, however, inevitably increases suspicion and fear, as division of peoples always does.

In the valley below the Shepherds' Fields, thousands of olive trees have been removed as the wall – a fence in some places – works its way around the West Bank. Part of the problem is the route the wall takes. It does not follow the 1949 'green line' but has incorporated significant portions of Palestinian Authority land. Fertile territory, such as that in the Cremasan Valley, loses its productivity as a buffer zone is established. The two cities of Jerusalem and Bethlehem are increasingly disconnected. The development of a new settlement in Givat Hamatos will completely cut off east Jerusalem from the southern West Bank.

In these circumstances it's no surprise that the proportion of Christians in the Palestinian Territories is diminishing, not because of any persecution from their Muslim neighbours but as a consequence of Christians having more Western contacts.

Educational opportunities, economic advancement and a freer life in the West attract the younger Christian generation. Who can blame them?

I think this is why the Shepherds' Fields now mean more to me than they did when I first visited them more than 30 years ago. In those days, although you knew there were tensions elsewhere, when you looked across the valley below, there were olive trees in abundance, and a sense of order and calm prevailed. Now the divisions are plain to see. Yet thousands of pilgrims come to this place to catch something of the joy, mystery and love of the Christ Child, Emmanuel, God with us.

At the Shepherds' Fields it seems to make entire sense that Jesus was not born in a place of stability, security, prosperity or freedom. Two thousand years ago he was born in occupied territory, in danger, away from home, with a manger for a cradle and the life of a refugee beckoning. It sounds agonizingly familiar. But that's the point. God reveals himself to us within the troubles of our world, not after our problems are solved. Jesus Christ is born in us when we are ill or while we are having a row, when we are divorced or when we are lonely. Christ comes to us in our dissatisfaction with life. He is with us in unemployment and grief. He is with us in our fear.

27

Jesus Christ is not a simple solution to the world's problems. The child born in Bethlehem grew to be a man who endured suffering, an unfair trial and an undeserved death. He knows life isn't fair. But in him God lives alongside us and within us, bringing us hope because even if we cannot love each other, he cannot stop loving us.

The first word the angel said to the shepherds was 'Fear not.' 'Don't worry.' They were the same words the angel spoke to Mary at the Annunciation – 'Don't be afraid.' They are the words of the angel to Joseph in his dream when he thinks of 'putting away' Mary because she is pregnant – 'Fear not.' In Antonio Barluzzi's chapel in the Shepherds' Fields, the three paintings are vivid in colour and full of movement. The first recalls the angels telling the shepherds of the birth of Jesus. The second pictures them at the stable where they find this newborn child. The third depicts them on their return journey, for Luke says, 'The shepherds returned, glorifying and praising God for all they had heard and seen ...' (Luke 2.20). Each of the scenes features a dog with the shepherds. The dog gets no mention in Luke's Gospel, but who is to say it wasn't there? The dog looks terrified in the first painting, attentive in the stable, and is clearly dancing with joy on the return journey, ears pricked up, caught in mid-bark and tail wagging. The shepherds and their dog return to work but are transformed. They face the same problems and live the same lives, but with new hope because of the joy of encountering Jesus Christ.

> *Come to us, Lord, when we are dissatisfied,*
> *fearful or quarrelsome, and help us to*
> *understand that you do not wait for our*
> *improvement but grace our unvarnished lives*
> *with your presence, love and blessing. Amen.*

5

Flinders Ranges, South Australia

Psalm 8.1–5

More than two-thirds of the Australian population live in major cities, and that proportion is growing. On my first visits to Australia, I spent most of my time in cities. Some friends in Adelaide suggested that an extended visit to the Flinders Ranges would ensure my experience was broadened. John Ruskin had a tendency to be so overcome with joy in nature that 'the presence of a Great and Holy Spirit' became obvious to him. I don't share that and find the Holy Spirit in human culture quite as much as in the natural world. But the Flinders Ranges lead me towards Ruskin's view more than almost anywhere else.

The Flinders Ranges date from the Cambrian period around 540 million years ago. Subsequent erosion has flattened some of the peaks, but the red and purple folds of the layers of rock convey a strong sense of their antiquity. Prior to the Cambrian period, living organisms on earth were generally very simple, composed of single cells. It was during the Cambrian age that life began to diversify. The fossil records show the growth of multicellular organisms, and thus the basis of subsequent animal life.

In the Flinders Ranges today, the geological formations simultaneously give the impression of taking you back to the dawn of time while appearing to have been created yesterday. The wildlife is varied. The sand ridges become more extensive the further north you travel, and barren salt lakes become more common. Before going there I had little idea that the Australian bush could be so beautiful.

The ranges are named after Matthew Flinders. European explorers found their way there in 1802 from HMS *Investigator*, the ship under the command of Matthew Flinders, which was the first to circumnavigate Australia. Human occupation, however, was well established tens of thousands of years earlier. The Adnyamathanha people (the word refers to people living in the hills or rocks) were the earliest settlers of the Flinders Ranges and their descendants still live in the area.

Aboriginal peoples tell creation stories. The sight of the Flinders Ranges made me understand why.

It was Jonathan Swift, clergyman and inventor of extraordinary worlds in *Gulliver's Travels*, who satirized the idea that 'the universe was formed by a fortuitous concourse of atoms'. He said, 'I will no more believe that than the accidental jumbling of the alphabet would fall into a most ingenious treatise of philosophy.' Aboriginal peoples may not have put it that way, but their rock paintings and sacred caves abound with testimony to their wonder at the order of the world in which they lived – as well as the struggle to survive.

For thousands of years the Adnyamathanha people told stories about the creation of their habitat in songs and legends and transmitted them orally from one generation to the next. Humankind, nature and the land were inseparable. The unity of creation was a repeated theme. So it is little surprise that European settlement of their land was regarded as a religious violation. It was an attack upon their identity. It was not so much a battle between two 'owners' of land as a dispute about the very nature of land itself.

Aboriginal peoples believe the ancient spirits gave them the land. Each people received their own area, and they celebrate this in song and dance. For such rituals their bodies are often decorated with seeds, feathers and red ochre, as they re-enact the deeds of the ancestral spirits who still travel with them. The fertility of the land and their own fertility come from the same source. It wasn't that the aboriginal peoples thought they owned the land. They believed the land owned them. And they still do.

The period when the earth and everything within it was created by their ancestral spirits is known by aboriginal peoples as 'The Dreaming' or 'Dreamtime'. Intriguingly, none of the many aboriginal languages contain a word for 'time' at all. So there is a sense in which the Dreamtime isn't isolated in the distant past when the world was made but is as contemporary as it is historic. Aboriginal peoples may use the term 'Dreaming' to refer to their contemporary life. The mythology of the past is lived in the life of the present. Dreaming is not simply stories but an understanding of the world as aboriginal peoples know it. It is a shield in times of need and a guide to daily life. No Christian familiar with the Old Testament should be surprised.

I once heard it argued that aboriginal beliefs were in stark contrast to Christianity. The speaker said that union with God and his perpetual blessing was a future promise, not a present reality. Heaven was a hope and we did not live in a perfect state of union with God now.

While it's true that our union with God in Christ is incomplete in this life, it seems a common misconception about the Christian religion that it is all future promise rather than present blessing. Perhaps one of the reasons why so many aboriginal peoples have embraced Christianity is that the Christian faith has enough immanence for it to be recognizable to them. And also enough that does not mistake life as we have it with life as God wants us to live it. In one of his books, Geoffrey Studdert-Kennedy wrote powerfully about our relationship with nature as fundamental to faith.

> No man or woman begins to live a full life
> until they realise they live in the presence
> of something greater [than] themselves.
> Wonder is at the base of true living, and
> wonder leads to worship ... then you
> begin to live more completely and realise
> the kinship between you and Nature ...
> out of Nature you came and are part and
> parcel with it. This brings us nearer faith ...
> reaching out to perfection.

The created order does, as Ruskin said, awaken a sense of 'the presence of a Great and Holy Spirit'. But it also leaves us longing for more. The 'more' is found in Jesus Christ.

God of time and space, Lord of the land,
Great and Holy Spirit, open our eyes to the
wonder of your creation and prevent us from
plundering and exploiting it. Amen.

6

St Benet's Abbey, Norfolk

John 6.10–14

O ne of the most surprising discoveries I made on becoming the Bishop of Norwich was that I was also the Abbot of St Benet's (apparently, having a wife and family did not disqualify me from the role). I soon learned that in 1536 King Henry VIII made William Rugge, then the Abbot of St Benet's, also the Bishop of Norwich, purloining a great deal of ecclesiastical revenue by doing so. However, he commanded him to continue to support the life of the monastery, situated nowadays in the parish of Horning on the Norfolk Broads, with 'twelve singing monks'. The likely explanation is that this was a relatively early stage in the dissolution of the monasteries and it was simply an expedient. Maintaining a monastery when the religious life had been destroyed everywhere in England proved impossible. Within a few years the community had ceased to exist.

St Benet's (a contraction of St Benedict's) seems to have been first founded as early as the end of the eighth century. Its home on the banks of the River Bure feels curiously remote even now. It is possible hermits lived on the site prior to the foundation of the abbey. Destroyed in the Viking invasions, the monastery was re-founded in the time of King Canute in 1020. It gradually became a stable and significant religious house.

It did have its ups and downs, however, as a visitation in 1494 reveals. Some of the monks complained they were overburdened with the recital of psalms, hymns and canticles, which didn't leave them enough time for anything else. It seems strange for Benedictine monks to complain about being in church too much, but the same visitation report states that the prior never went to services at all, that the singing monks chattered instead of being silent when in choir, and the younger monks were rude and cheeky to their elders and betters. Whenever we dig deep into the past, we realize that it is both a foreign country, and peopled by human beings like ourselves.

Fresh interest was taken in St Benet's Abbey in Victorian times. The Revd Arthur Brown was the Vicar of Dilham about a dozen miles distant from St Benet's. In 1872 he published *The Last of the Abbots.*

It enlivens the historical details with a great many imaginary conversations. The author took delight that in the Bishop of Norwich of his time 'we have an Abbot among us in these degenerate days, the last of a long, long line!' He goes on to say, 'Well would it become him, as Lord still of the soil, to save from further desecration the spot where the ashes have been deposited of many generations of monks, and of not a few of England's notabilities.' Among those 'notabilities' was Sir John Falstolf, buried near the high altar in 1459, the nobleman who built Caister Castle and upon whom Shakespeare's Falstaff was based.

Decades after Arthur Brown wrote his book, the then Bishop of Norwich began to conduct occasional open-air services at the site of the abbey. From the 1950s onwards this became an annual event on the first Sunday in August. A Norfolk wherry conveys the bishop/abbot to the site and hundreds of people gather for an ecumenical service near the site of the high altar. In the early 1980s the Brethren of St Benet's were established – local men who were part of the worshipping life of the churches in the area and who meet each month for fellowship, study and prayer, often singing Compline at the conclusion of their time together. The site itself is now owned and managed by the Norfolk Archaeological Trust and a group of Friends maintain interest in it.

Since the ruins are so modest, it seems surprising that there is such renewed interest, spiritual as well as archaeological. The location does, however, seem sanctified by prayer from centuries past and is one where distractions are few. Among the many people who come to the annual August service are those who have visited St Benet's on a quiet weekday and feel compelled to return. Almost every year after the service, someone has told me a personal story of perplexity, distress, sorrow or brokenness which they have brought to this windy, open and exposed place. Sometimes we seem to need shrines where we are enveloped by protective sacred walls. There are none at St Benet's Abbey. This is a sacred space without walls where there is nowhere to hide away. Perhaps that is its special value.

More than once I have found myself preaching at St Benet's on the feeding of the five thousand, possibly because water is nearby and hundreds of people are sitting on the green grass. At the end of the feeding miracle in John's Gospel, Jesus instructs the disciples to 'gather up the fragments that remain, so that nothing may be lost' (John 6.12). Just a few physical fragments of St Benet's Abbey survive. It saw several episodes of destruction over the centuries. Even its dissolution was fragmented, and in some senses is still incomplete.

39

Church buildings in gleaming condition with flour-ishing and successful congregations may not always be inviting for those who are broken in spirit. Yet it is the fragments of our lives, the insecurities, the unre-solved tensions, the wounded limbs and the pierced hearts that Jesus takes to himself when he gathers the fragments that remain. Jesus Christ, broken for us on the Cross, gives us his broken body in the sac-rament of the Eucharist. He takes our brokenness into himself by sharing the fragmentation of our lives, and becomes the means of our own wholeness and healing. Our fragmentation is often the result of our sins. Christ's sharing in our life is the conse-quence of his love.

I began my visits to St Benet's Abbey thinking of it as a historical curiosity. I have come to appreciate it as a spiritual gift to the broken and weary in heart.

> *Bless, Lord, the brokenness of our lives by*
> *gathering the fragments of our frailty to*
> *yourself, so that we may find in you rest for*
> *our weariness and hope for our fears. Amen.*

7

Center Parcs, Longleat

Matthew 14.22–33

On holiday, when our children were young, at Center Parcs, Longleat, I was persuaded to climb high above the swimming pool to slide down a long twisty tube into the water below. Sitting on the edge before pushing myself off, I was surprised to find traffic lights. They changed from red to green to tell you when to thrust yourself forward. Suddenly Sóren Kierkegaard came into my mind. He talked about the leap of faith being like launching out over seventy thousand fathoms. I felt fairly sure that Kierkegaard never sat on the edge of a flume. Then the light went from red to green. Kierkegaard vanished from my mind as my body hurtled helplessly downwards.

At the bottom my arms and legs were flailing underwater. Then I discovered that the pool into which I had been deposited was only about two or three feet deep. I stood up, glad to be alive. Kierkegaard sneered at those who just like to paddle in the shallow end of Christianity. As I stood there, another thought came to my mind. This was just like baptism, plunging into the waters of Christ's death to rise with him to new life. I had a little theological experience, then, at both ends of the Center Parcs' flume at Longleat. It didn't appear that anyone else around me was much engaged in theological speculation. Perhaps it's an occupational hazard for the ordained.

There is something appropriate about Kierkegaard causing moments of strange illumination in unlikely circumstances long after his death. He maintained that his role was to be an irritant and a corrective, a pinch of pepper in the stew, to spark response and to flavour life. Born in 1813 in Copenhagen, Sóren grew up in a wealthy family, but his father, a devout Lutheran, was a tormented man. He believed his family's life was under some sort of divine curse. It was incapacitating for Sóren, his seventh and last child (only one of Kierkegaard's older siblings lived into adulthood).

When he was 25, Kierkegaard's father died and his young son became so rich he never needed to work for a living again. Rather than encouraging a dissolute life, this good fortune seemed to spur Kierkegaard into intense activity. He completed his university degree and within a few years published his first book, a fierce critique of the work of Hans Christian Andersen.

In September 1840, Kierkegaard announced his engagement to Regine Olsen, a lively and intelligent daughter of a very senior Danish civil servant. At the same time, Kierkegaard began his preparation to become a Lutheran pastor. It looked as if his life was on course for a steady future.

A year later he broke off the engagement. He still loved Regine (and she did all that she could to win him back) but he believed it to be a necessary decision. It seemed as if he could not inflict his melancholy upon the one he loved. But a greater cause of the break-up was Kierkegaard's unique sense of his vocation. He believed his insight was so exceptional that he couldn't share his life intimately with anyone. He was called to a lonely and isolated existence, no longer to be a Lutheran pastor nor to make allowances for a wife, but to write, speak and think the truth to a world which did not want to hear what he had to say. If no one wanted to read his books, it did not matter since he did not write for money.

Kierkegaard's books all illustrate, if obliquely at first, the need for redemption through the incarnate God of Christian faith. But much of the time his target is the prevailing philosophy of his age. He ridicules contemporary philosophy even when he attempts to explain to Regine why he broke off their engagement. In *Either/Or* (Kierkegaard did not go in for snappy titles) he writes this:

> If you marry, you will regret it; if you do not marry, you will also regret it; whether you marry or do not marry, you will regret both ... believe a woman and you will regret it; believe her not, you will also regret that; whether you believe a woman or believe her not, you will regret it ... this, gentlemen, is the sum and substance of all philosophy ...

It may sound a bit mad to us. As an explanation to a jilted fiancée it seems lacking in emotional insight. At the time, Hegel was the dominant intellectual influence in Danish and German philosophy and theology. For Hegel, history was God's autobiography. God was not a transcendent being in a separate sphere beyond space and time. He was more like the soul of the world. All truth could be discovered within a philosophy which presented a comprehensive account of all reality.

Kierkegaard did not think that God could be included within a single explanation of the cosmos. That would seem to make God subservient to German philosophy. So Kierkegaard goads Hegelians. As he does so he reflects on the way human beings are often regretful, even despairing of whatever they have done, no matter what the circumstances of their lives. The breaking of his engagement to Regine is part of this. Kierkegaard did not believe the world was objectively improving.

There is an absolute distinction in Kierkegaard's theology between God and the human. He believed his contemporaries tried to tame God by incorporating him into their civil and ecclesiastical establishments. Kierkegaard thought the radical difference between God and human beings was so great as to make any communication between them impossible. And yet that impossibility becomes real in Jesus. It is only the figure of Jesus Christ who enables any communication between God and humanity. It is God who does the impossible by reaching out to us.

Kierkegaard hated Christianity-made-easy. In the Gospels there is no universal recognition by the world of the power of Jesus. Instead, there was scandal and offence, since Jesus faced charges of blasphemy and suffered crucifixion. People could see

45

Jesus on the Cross but refused to acknowledge what was happening before their very eyes. Kierkegaard wrote, 'The only cure for despair is the "leap of faith" whereby trust in the infinite possibility of God brings about authentic existence.' In other words, the leap of faith is not a religious abstraction. It is a leap of faith into one's authentic self. It is the discovery of who I am, as well as of who God is. Which takes me back to Center Parcs and plunging down the flume. I read a lot of Kierkegaard after that holiday. Since Kierkegaard had so little time for bishops and the established Church, he might even have smiled at the irony.

> *Eternal God, as you reach out to us in Jesus Christ, may we dare to take a leap of faith towards you, today and every day. Amen.*

8

Leptis Magna, Libya

Hebrews 11.8–16

O ne of the best-preserved Roman cities in the world is at Leptis Magna about 80 miles east of Tripoli. For 900 years the city lay under sand and was forgotten. The Italian conquest of Libya in the early twentieth century led to its rediscovery. Leptis Magna has never been easy for the independent traveller to reach, and since the fall of Colonel Gaddafi nearly all its visitors have been local. During the 2011 Libyan civil war it was claimed that Leptis Magna was being used by pro-Gaddafi groups as a location for military hardware. NATO officials then refused to rule out air strikes if the claim proved to be true. By the end of 2016 there were reports of Libyan civilians forming their own civil defence force around the archaeological ruins – a huge task since Leptis covers an area of about 120 acres. They feared that Islamic militants would be intent on destroying some of the most important surviving buildings from the Roman Empire.

I have visited Leptis Magna twice. Its location on the Mediterranean coast is stunningly beautiful but it takes a leap of imagination to comprehend why it rose to such importance. Originally founded from Carthage in the seventh century BC, the settlement remained a Carthaginian outpost until the end of the Third Punic War (AD 146). Even then its incorporation into imperial Rome was slow. It was given first the status of a *civitas libera et immunis* (a free and immune city), which had all the hallmarks of an independent life since no tribute was paid to Rome.

As time went on, Leptis became increasingly strategically important, a port valued because of the vast amount of olive oil produced in the fertile land that surrounded it. By 46 BC a tax of three million pounds of olive oil annually had to be paid to Rome by Leptis Magna, an indication of its growing wealth and increasing population. The next few centuries saw Leptis at the height of its influence, the third city of North Africa after Carthage and Alexandria.

Leptis Magna was the birthplace of Septimius Severus, the Roman Emperor from AD 193 to 211, and the founder of the Severan dynasty. His military successes brought him the imperial crown, since he was effectively declared emperor by his troops. His victories over the Parthians (whose empire had its centre in modern Iran) were celebrated architecturally in Rome. The Triumphal Arch of Septimius Severus to the north-west of the Roman Forum ensures his name survives to this day.

To my mind, an even more impressive triumphal arch is the one in Leptis Magna, which marks both his Parthian victories but also his return to his home city in 203. It is a freestanding four-way arch with eight Corinthian columns. Four frieze panels depict the imperial family triumphant in military victory and civic life. Even the location of the triumphal arch in Leptis Magna signifies the power of the home-grown Emperor. It's placed at the crossroads of the city's two most significant roads – the *cardo*, which runs from north to south, and the *decimanus maximus*, running from east to west.

The arch was discovered by the archaeologist Giacomo Guidi in the 1920s. The base below the level of the sand was intact, but the arches themselves had fallen many centuries earlier. A complete restoration was effected, something archaeologists nowadays would probably be loath to do, but which gives an unmistakeable impression of the grandeur and the power of the Severan dynasty.

What is unusual about Leptis Magna is that no new city has ever been built on the ruins. By the sixth century Leptis was entirely Christian. Some new churches were built but generally old buildings were adapted for Christian use. By then the population had declined significantly. The city was largely abandoned by the time of the Arab conquest in the mid-seventh century. It never revived. By 1000 Leptis Magna had completely disappeared beneath the sand.

To visit Leptis Magna is to be reminded both of the sophistication and architectural magnificence of the ancient world and of the transience of human power. This is often more obscure at other sites because of later adaptations by succeeding generations. The impermanence of even the greatest imperial powers and the passing of civilizations leaves a deep impression. Plato believed the human instinct to found cities came as a result of our need for collective protection against wild beasts and marauders. Aristotle thought the creation of the city was the consequence of our social instincts. Both are probably true, and yet Leptis Magna was also a place to leave behind, as Septimius Severus did, if ambitions on the largest scale were to be realized or the world was to be changed.

The call of God to the patriarchs caused them to leave their homes and cities to follow where the Lord led. Abraham, Isaac and Jacob did not stay where they were. In Hebrews 13.14 we are told, 'here we have no abiding city'. A succession of heroes of the faith are recalled in Hebrews 11–12, a great list of those who 'wandered in deserts and mountains, hiding in caves and holes in the ground'. The writer of the Letter to the Hebrews says it is in leaving or being displaced from home that our spiritual ancestors discovered God calling them beyond their ordinary existence.

It seems to be assumed in much of our public discourse that our cities, and Western civilization – even what it means to be British – have some God-given permanence. Ours is a civilization which will pass just as surely as Leptis Magna was covered by sand. The point of visiting these ancient sites is to enter sympathetically into another period of history but also to be reminded of the impermanence of our own.

My recollections of Leptis Magna have become more vivid in recent years, knowing that from that coastline in North Africa many thousands of refugees and migrants have fled to Europe to seek a better life. The heroes of faith described in the Letter to the Hebrews 'were strangers and foreigners on the

51

earth ... seeking a homeland ... they desire a better country, that is a heavenly one. Therefore God is not ashamed to be called their God; indeed, he has prepared a city for them' (Hebrews 11.13–16). Today's refugees from North Africa are often desperate, but like many before them, they travel in hope too.

> *God of history, as civilizations grow and fade,*
> *give us a sense of perspective, that we may find*
> *our security in you, knowing that we are all*
> *strangers and pilgrims on this earth. Amen.*

9

The Woolsack, House of Lords

Hebrews 1.1–3

Sometime in the fourteenth century, King Edward III suggested that the Lord Chancellor should preside over the upper house of parliament by sitting on a large bale of wool. The wool trade was then of central importance to the economy and well-being of England. Once traditions are established in parliament, there is rarely a rush to change them. So today in front of the Throne in the Chamber of the House of Lords there remains a very large square cushion stuffed with wool and covered in red cloth. It's called the Woolsack.

The Lord Chancellor sat there to preside over the House of Lords until 2006, when that function of the Lord Chancellor's office was removed and a Lord Speaker was elected by members of the House. Whenever guests come to observe proceedings they frequently comment on the silence

of the Lord Speaker. It is certainly a contrast to
what happens in the House of Commons, where
the Speaker not only calls people to speak, but rules
on points of order and 'Mr Speaker' is addressed by
members in their speeches. It is entirely different in
the upper house. The Lord Speaker does formally
put questions before votes are taken, announces
the results of a division and sometimes makes
announcements, e.g. the death of a member. But,
in a self-regulating house, members are meant to
manage proceedings themselves without interven-
tions from the chair. When two or more people
are attempting to speak at the same time, it is the
Leader of the House who has to sort it out. The
Lord Speaker remains silent even then. Nor do the
members address the Lord Speaker; they speak to
the whole House instead, beginning with the traditional 'My Lords ...'

Over the years I have grown to value the silent
Lord Speaker for reasons quite unconnected with
the office. In the grandeur of the Lords' Chamber,
with its overdose of gold leaf, the modest powers of
the presiding figure convey more than words may.
There is something ecclesiastical in the character
of the surroundings, so it's perhaps not surprising that the setting prompts theological reflection, particularly about speech and silence. There

is very little silence in the Chamber. The speeches are many, yet rarely heard from the Woolsack. The Lord Speaker does give an address, though, at great events, such as the occasions when Pope Benedict or President Obama spoke to both houses of parliament in Westminster Hall. On those occasions it was clear that the Lord Speaker embodied the House of Lords. The Lord Speaker also leads the outreach programme to schools, universities and other institutions, seeking to spread understanding of the work of parliament and of the upper house in particular.

Knowing there is a time to speak and a time to keep silence has echoes of the Preacher's words in Ecclesiastes. However, it's the opening of the Letter to the Hebrews which best expresses the relationship between speech and silence.

> Long ago God spoke to our ancestors in
> many and various ways by the prophets, but
> in these last days he has spoken to us by a
> Son, whom he appointed heir of all things,
> through whom he also created the worlds.
> He is the reflection of God's glory and the
> exact imprint of God's very being, and he
> sustains all things by his powerful word.
> (Hebrews 1.1–3)

Although God speaks to us in Jesus Christ he does not do so only through words. For the first 30 years of his earthly life we have no record of the words spoken by Jesus, even when we are told that he spoke with such authority in the temple at the age of 12. While the teaching of Jesus recorded in the Gospels has generated a mountain of literature, countless sermons and plenty of disputed opinions, there is surprisingly little of it compared with the legacy of the central figure in many other world religions. It was once estimated that all of the incidents recorded in the Gospels could be packed into three weeks of intense activity. That gives an indication of just how many of the words of Jesus have not been preserved. But it isn't his words upon which we rely for our salvation. It is Jesus Christ living with us and among us, as he promised after his resurrection. 'I am with you always, to the end of time' (Matthew 28.20). While many Christians hear Christ speak to them in different ways, it is often his silent presence in our lives which is most powerful. We have much to learn in silent communion, just as couples in love find that the chatter of their early relationship is gradually replaced by a depth too great for words. Perhaps that is why James tells us in his letter, 'be quick to listen, slow to speak' (James 1.19). In iconography, saints are frequently depicted with very small mouths but large ears, reflecting this teaching.

In Thomas Hardy's novel *Under the Greenwood Tree* there is a conversation between two country people about a third, Geoffrey Day. One of them attests, 'Geoffrey Day is a clever man if ever there was one. Never says anything: not he.' The other says, 'Ay; one o' these up-country London ink-bottle chaps would call Geoffrey a fool.' Then they agree that 'he can keep silence well. That man's silence is wonderful to listen to.' They go on to emphasize that 'every moment of it is brimmen over wi' sound understanding'.

It is a touching scene and scarcely anything could be more different from the spirit of our own age, marked by such a plethora of words on the airwaves, in texting, tweeting and in print. But do they carry more authority as they proliferate?

Jesus is economical in his use of words and in very little rush. He leaves crowds to go off to lonely places to pray. He waits, patiently, in the Garden of Gethsemane before his betrayal and arrest. He is silent before braying crowds calling for Pontius Pilate to crucify him. Perhaps seeing everything in the context of eternity generated the right pace at which to live and a capacity to cherish both speech and silence.

The grandeur of the Chamber of the House of Lords is intended to impress by its scale, majesty

57

and authority. Yet a bale of wool, and a largely silent Lord Speaker as the focus of day-to-day authority, may have much to teach us in the jabbering wordiness of contemporary life.

Word of God, give us the wisdom to know when to speak and when to refrain from speaking, so that both in silence and in utterance we may honour you. Amen.

10

Christ the Redeemer, Corcovado, Rio de Janeiro

John 12.32

The local people of Rio (known locally as Cariocas) like to claim that after God made the world in six days and rested on the seventh, he went to work again on the eighth day to create Rio de Janeiro. They can be forgiven their hyperbole, since there is scarcely an oceanfront in the world to match Rio's. Its long stretches of sandy beaches, set in Guanabara Bay, are in stark contrast to the surrounding mountains, green with forest and jungle, and with birds, butterflies and flowers in profusion. The Sugar Loaf Mountain rises vertically from the bay and the cable car to get there is one of the most thrilling rides in the world.

Below the Sugar Loaf these glorious gifts of nature are further embellished by the culture, arts, music and personalities of the Brazilian people. Copacabana and Ipanema are perhaps the best-known beaches in the world and graced by some of the world's most beautiful people. Rio began its rapid growth in the eighteenth century during Brazil's gold rush. When in 1808 the King of Portugal fled to Rio (taking his court with him) to avoid Napoleon's armies, the thousands of people who accompanied him began to create in Rio a European city with parks, promenades and palaces. By the end of the nineteenth century it was one of the largest cities in the world.

In the latter half of the twentieth century, São Paulo overtook Rio to become Brazil's greatest industrial city, while the seat of government was moved inland to Brasilia. For a time Rio lost self-confidence, not least because its streets became a byword for violence and robbery. In more recent decades this has changed, well reflected in Rio being chosen as the host city for the Olympics in 2016, following closely on the Brazilian World Cup two years earlier. Sweeping views of Rio introduced the Olympic highlights on television every day. They invariably featured the huge statue of Christ the Redeemer at the top of the Corcovado Mountain. It stands almost one hundred feet tall and weighs over six hundred tons. It has been declared as one of the New Seven Wonders of the World.

I may have missed descriptions or discussions about the statue of Christ the Redeemer in the Olympic coverage but I can scarcely recall it being mentioned. It is visible all over Rio and is the most unmistakeable manmade structure to be found in the city. Perhaps it was left unmentioned because in our secular culture it was hard to explain. Even so, the image of Jesus Christ, arms outstretched, redeeming the world and reigning over the city, was there in almost every panoramic shot. No words were really needed. Perhaps the statue fulfilled at the Olympics the intentions of those who conceived it more effectively than they had ever dreamed. It was completed in 1931, partly as an attempt by local Catholics to reclaim Rio from the godless materialism which they believed to be undermining its life. It is intriguing how previous ages, which we now consider as pious because of the extent of churchgoing, did not regard themselves as such at the time.

I first visited Rio in 1990 when the then Archbishop of Canterbury, Robert Runcie, made a lengthy visit to the Anglican churches in South America. It included the ordination of the first Uruguayan Anglican priest and the consecration of the Anglican cathedral in Asunción in Paraguay. Quiet and understated work by the Anglican Church was being done in many South American countries.

A visit to Cardinal Arns in São Paulo for an ecumenical service was memorable since the cathedral was crowded with the desperately poor. Those influenced by liberation theology who were engaged in building base communities had a striking humility. By contrast, the statue of Christ the Redeemer in Rio seemed to reflect an earlier and triumphalist Catholicism. My first impressions were unfavourable, for it appeared to convey an image of a Christ who kept his distance, presiding over creation rather than immersed within it. John Stott, the doyen of Anglican evangelical preachers in the twentieth century, once told a story of a man from the favelas of Rio who climbed the Corcovado Mountain to plead with Christ, 'Don't stay away from us; live among us and give us new faith in you.' John Stott said that a distant God was a terrible caricature 'which the Cross smashes to smithereens ... the God who allows us to suffer, once suffered himself in Christ, and continues to suffer with us and for us today'.

But even on that first visit I was struck by the way in which the arms of Christ the Redeemer seemed to embrace the whole city. Quite how a sculpture of that size can be both majestic and tender at the same time is a mystery, but that's part of its glory. New residents in Rio speak of the way the statue acts as both a beacon and a marker. They always know where they are in relation to Christ the Redeemer.

Who can say how far geographical dependence leads to spiritual awakening?

Hundreds of thousands of people make the pilgrimage up the Corcovado Mountain each year. I've done so myself on each of three visits to Rio. The closer you get to the statue the more enormous it seems. Yet that perspective is lost when you stand at the base. You then realize you can scarcely see the figure of Christ at all. In 2006 a chapel in the statue base was dedicated by the Cardinal Archbishop of Rio. Mass is celebrated there and baptisms and marriages take place too.

When we are 'in Christ', to use St Paul's distinctive phrase, we do not see Christ as separate from us. We are taken up in him. That, I believe, has been one of the gifts of Christ the Redeemer to me and countless others who have reached the top of the Corcovado Mountain over the years. We can be drawn to the majestic Christ at a distance. Once we are embraced by his open arms and taken into his life, we cannot see ourselves as separate from him. Christ reaches out to us and takes us to himself. That's redemption.

> *Christ our redeemer, your arms were opened wide upon the cross; hold us in the embrace of your sacrificial love, so that we may be one with you now and in all eternity. Amen.*

11

Bishop Bridge, Norwich

Ephesians 3.18–21

The River Wensum cuts through the centre of Norwich, but only one medieval bridge survives. Bishop Bridge dates from 1340, but is now closed to vehicles though it still fulfils its original purpose for thousands of pedestrians and cyclists every week. It leads into Bishopgate and until the end of the eighteenth century there was a fortified gate at the western end of the bridge. Bishopgate continues to the old Bishop's Palace and the modern Bishop's House, which was built adjacent to its predecessor.

An enterprising photographer once sent me a computerized image of Bishop Bridge overlain with hundreds of pictures of me in a mitre. Intended to amuse, it achieved that aim but also prompted reflection on the nature of a bishop's task.

One of the less frequently used terms for a bishop nowadays is 'pontiff'. The Pope continues to be described as the Supreme Pontiff, though such nomenclature does not find much favour with Pope Francis. A Pontifical Mass is one celebrated by any bishop and is a term still sometimes used in the higher reaches of the Church of England. In the state religion of ancient Rome, a pontiff or pontifex was a member of the principal college of priests. The Christian Church adapted the terminology, perhaps because of its Latin meaning. *Pons* is bridge and *fex* comes from the Latin *facere*, meaning 'to make'. A pontiff or pontifex is thus a bridge builder. The vocation of a bishop is to build bridges between the local and universal church, between the Church and the world she serves, between people in different institutions and groups, all in the name of Jesus Christ who bridges the chasm between us and God.

There is no explicit mention of bridges anywhere in the Bible. I have heard it claimed this is deliberate, since God divides seas rather than builds bridges, and the Christian life is one of negotiating the stormy waters of suffering rather than making bridges over them. The lack of reference to bridges is surprising given that the Romans were such great bridge builders. St Paul might have warmed to such a metaphor, but we've no indication he did so, though it's been used countless times in later Christian centuries.

Bridges both create connections and carry loads. Bishop Bridge in Norwich is an arch bridge, a type favoured by the Romans. Although relatively modest in size, it has no fewer than three arches. To give it a Trinitarian interpretation may be fanciful, but Leonardo da Vinci's definition of an arch bears repetition.

> An arch is nothing else than a strength
> caused by two weaknesses; for the arch in
> buildings is made up of two segments of a
> circle, and each of these segments being in
> itself very weak desires to fall, and as one
> withstands the downfall of the other, the
> two weaknesses are converted into a single
> strength.

Walking over Bishop Bridge in Norwich (as I do on the way to the railway station or the football ground), the shared weaknesses of the arches beneath me act as a strength. They have carried loads for the better part of seven hundred years. They provide me with a reminder of interdependence within the body of Christ.

Yet it is hard to walk across Bishop Bridge without recognizing that some who crossed it in earlier centuries were going to their deaths. The Lollards' Pit, a fairly busy place of execution in the fifteenth and sixteenth centuries, was situated beside it. No one knows quite how many people met their death by burning here. In 1428 a priest called William White, who preached against abuses in the Church and advocated the need for an English Bible, was brought here with two other followers of John Wycliffe (known as Lollards) to be burned for heresy.

Thomas Bilney, born near Dereham and a man of great learning, met a fiery end here in 1531. The pit was used most frequently during the reign of Mary Tudor, when up to 50 Protestants were burned. After the accession of Queen Elizabeth I it fell into disuse. A public house called 'Lollards Pit' on the site keeps its memory alive, though it is doubtful that many of those who died in the pit were particularly fond of alehouses.

This tragic history beside Bishop Bridge is a reminder of the inhumanity with which Christians once treated each other. They did so because they thought matters of eternal salvation were at stake. Perhaps in our own age it is our spiritual carelessness rather than conviction that has made us more charitable. Even so, the arches of the Bishop Bridge seem to rebuke such an exercise of naked power. Burnings were not a consequence of Leonardo's understanding of two weaknesses making a strength. His vision suggested instead the need to build spiritual bridges. Perhaps there is much to be said for a weaker Church, a more humble Christian community, a Church stripped of worldly power. Such a Church may be better at constructing arches and building bridges, and better able to understand why St Paul said that when he was weak, then he was strong.

One of the surprising features of Paul's letters is that he seems to be at his most confident in Christ during his most vulnerable moments. It is when he is a prisoner and facing the fiercest opposition that his prayer for the Church becomes most eloquent. This is when he prays that his brothers and sisters may comprehend 'the breadth, the length and height and depth and to know the love of Christ that surpasses knowledge'. He gives a testimony, too, that through Christ those who follow him are 'able to accomplish abundantly far more than all we can ask or imagine' (Ephesians 3.18–20). In the arch of the Church our weaknesses become a strength, but only if we support each other.

Bishop Bridge, Norwich

*Lord Jesus Christ, you support us in our
weakness so that we find new strength in you.
Give us the capacity to bear the stresses and
tensions of others, that they may also come to
know you, the Saviour of all. Amen.*

12

St Enodoc's Church, Cornwall

Jeremiah 29.11–13

There may be no other church entirely surrounded by a golf course but that is not St Enodoc's main claim to fame. Many visitors come to Trebetherick near Polzeath on the north Cornish coast to pay pilgrimage to Sir John Betjeman, who lies buried in the churchyard. There is a memorial inside the church to his father Ernest Betjeman, while his mother Mabel is also buried in the churchyard. The Betjeman family (John was an only child) used to travel to the area for their holidays from north London on the Atlantic Coast Express, now long disappeared. The impact of those weeks was indelible. The north Cornish coast, steam trains, Edwardian villas, an English country church: they were among the passions which caught Betjeman's imagination for the rest of his life.

St Enodoc's Church naturally kindles the imagination because of its setting and also its story. Unusual among Cornish churches since it has a spire, it sits in a hollow. The church disappears into the landscape from some angles, while from others the top of the spire emerges uncannily from the golf links. The spire bends over at the top, leading to comparisons with a dunce's cap, but is perhaps better described as nodding in sympathy and understanding. Worshippers still walk across the fairways to Evensong on a Sunday afternoon, just as Betjeman himself did. His poem 'Sunday Afternoon Service in St Enodoc Church, Cornwall' written in 1944 begins: 'Come on! Come on!' The poet tells us it is five to three and if his party do not get a move on the priest will have intoned, 'Dearly beloved brethren …' before they get there. Evensong at St Enodoc's is still at 3 p.m. Some continuities in the Church of England are very reassuring.

But why is the hamlet of St Enodoc there at all? There seems never to have been a substantial community, but enough people lived there in the twelfth century to build the church, perhaps to replace an earlier one marking the site where the hermit, Enodoc, may once have lived. We know nothing of St Enodoc himself, though the monks of Bodmin venerated him in medieval times. Perhaps even by then they may not have known much about him.

St Enodoc's is one of many Cornish places dedicated to saints from the Celtic past about whom nothing is known other than their names. If, as seems possible, the church is set near Enodoc's hermit cave from centuries past, then the ongoing worship in this church offers a continuity of praise to God which is as inspiring as its setting. No wonder John Betjeman found a poetic impulse here.

No one knows when the sand dunes gradually claimed the church, but sometime in the eighteenth century it disappeared almost entirely from view. It must have been as much the consequence of neglect as of nature. At one stage, the interior could only be accessed through the roof. The incumbent did this on an annual basis to hold a service with the parish sexton. This may sound an admirable way of sustaining Christian worship in an inaccessible place, but it is rather more likely that it was not deep devotion which drove it. Rather it was the minimum necessary to keep the church open as a place of worship and so to claim the tithes.

The Victorian renewal of the Church of England saved St Enodoc's. For over a decade from 1853, the vicar of the parish, Hart Smith, supervised a gradual but complete restoration. The sand was removed, the roof repaired, foundations strengthened and the churchyard protected with a wall, keeping the sand out and the graves clear. It was a slow and painstaking business. Hart Smith's son explained that it was all done 'by the masons and workmen of the parish with loving care, and nothing was destroyed needlessly or removed if it was of use or of interest'. Even today, St Enodoc's seems to have been restored rather more sympathetically than some other Cornish churches were at the time.

The gradual rebirth of St Enodoc's means that features of the church remain that survived through at least a century of burial under the sand. The font, for example, is Norman. The incised effigies of John Mably and his daughter, which date from 1687, were rescued and are now to be found in the south porch. By the seventeenth century a rather primitive incised slab as a memorial was unusual. Such things could have been easily discarded in a less sympathetic restoration.

Rebirth in the Christian tradition is sometimes regarded as a sudden experience. Being 'born again' can be dramatic. More commonly, however, rebirth in Christ is gradual; an awakening, a discovery which takes time. John Betjeman said the sort of conversion experience St Paul had on the road to Damascus was not one with which he was familiar.

However, he described conversion memorably as 'turning round, to gaze upon a love profound'. Betjeman's own experience of faith was not one with blinding lights but 'a fitful glow', and sometimes not even that. Even so, it was Betjeman's conviction that when the light of faith went out completely you needed to be resolute enough to go to worship 'in God's house below – my parish church'. And so he did at St Enodoc's.

Betjeman was one of countless seekers over the years who have found their way to this little reborn church. Many of us need to be born again very frequently. Jesus gave us the sacrament of Holy Communion to aid the regular rekindling of our faith in him, looking to a time when we shall see God in all his glory. The sacraments are not for the super-certain, but to kindle the embers of faith. St Enodoc's church, nestling in the hollow of the golf links, surrounded by tamarisk, and with its own history of rebirth, is also a sacramental sign, pointing beyond itself to Jesus Christ. John Betjeman's poem on the conversion of St Paul concludes with both honest reflection and a longing for the divine light.

> What is conversion? Turning round
> to gaze upon a love profound.
> For some of us see Jesus plain

and never once look back again,
and some of us have seen and known
and turned and gone away alone,
but most of us turn slow to see
the figure hanging on a tree
and stumble on and blindly grope
upheld by intermittent hope.
God grant before we die we all
may see the light as did St Paul.

13

Holborn Underground Station

2 Corinthians 9.8, 9

As I stepped on to a rising escalator at Holborn Underground Station, a woman turned round and without any greeting asked me, 'Do you think you should get compassionate leave from work when your partner dies?' I blinked and said I thought there were laws about this sort of thing, but yes, I was sure a good employer would be sympathetic. 'Well, my partner died yesterday and my boss says I have to come in to work.' I expressed my sympathies. We exchanged a few more sentences and when we reached the top she said, 'Would you give me a blessing?' I laid my hands on this woman's head while people barged past, said a prayer and gave her God's blessing. She looked up, smiled and walked off saying, 'I feel better now. I never expected that.'

I have no idea who she was (she did not want to give her name) or what has happened since. But it was a couple of minutes of intense connection with someone who seemed to be the victim of a total lack of compassion. Whenever I change trains at Holborn I think about the incident, and ponder one of the beatitudes – 'Blessed are those who mourn, for they shall be comforted' (Matthew 5.4).

I doubt we would have had this conversation if we had just passed on the street. Clearly my clerical collar, and perhaps my pectoral cross too, were taken as signs of potential pastoral sympathy. I was 'open for business'. There seemed something, too, in the fact that we were travelling together, even if for a very short journey.

That brief experience at Holborn Underground Station led me to suggest 'Unexpected Blessings' as the theme for an annual art prize sponsored at the Norwich University of the Arts. There is always a theme with scriptural reference but which is open to wider interpretation too.

The brief produced an exhibition of exceptional quality. The winner was an arrangement of a collection of handwritten letters cast in solid bronze and simply called *Epistle*. The young artist wanted to emphasize the high value now placed on the weight of the handwritten letter. It has become a special blessing in an age in which such letters are much rarer. The title of the work – *Epistle* – captured also the way in which so much Christian scripture consists of letters, read again and again over the centuries.

Soon after giving this award I found myself expected to preach on a passage from the first epistle of John: 'Do not love the world or the things in the world' (1 John 2.15). It seems a very striking contrast to the message of John's Gospel, where we read, 'God so loved the world that he gave his only Son, so that everyone who believes in him may not perish but have eternal life' (John 3.16).

They seem to present very different biblical attitudes to the world, despite both coming from the Johannine tradition. In the first, the world with its desires of the flesh and pride in riches is a distraction from the gospel. It is a world in its final period of history. In his letter John says, 'We know that it is the last hour.' The first letter of John, probably written towards the end of the first century, comes from a time when the Church is small and experiencing persecution. The task of the Christian was to remain faithful, cherish the knowledge and love of God, believe in the

forgiveness of sins, and develop the will and capacity to resist evil.

Yet in John's Gospel we learn that God so loved the
world – this world full of the desires of the flesh, and
pride in riches – that he sent his only Son to live and
die in it. When reading that God so loved the world,
we are transported back to the book of Genesis,
where our creator God looks upon the world and
sees that it is very good. The world is God's. It
does not belong to the evil one. God blesses us in
the world. That does not mean we do not know
what a hostile world is like, as the first letter of John
describes. But God blesses us in our perplexities and
confusions, just as I believe he did for that stranger
at Holborn tube station.

It is a world of unexpected blessings. I seem to
experience quite a lot of them on trains or in the
underground. When I was travelling into London
from Norwich one day, the train in front had broken down and all its passengers joined us. Our train
became exceptionally full. I sneezed. The woman sitting next to me said, 'Bless you', then turned to look
at me and for the first time saw my purple shirt and
clerical collar. She immediately said, 'I'm sorry.' She
clearly thought she had trespassed on my professional
territory. I told her I was into receiving unexpected

blessings. A conversation about faith and her longing for it ensued, which would not have happened had I not sneezed.

On a separate occasion I was travelling on the Circle Line on an extremely hot summer's day. I removed my clerical collar and opened the top button of my shirt, also taking off my pectoral cross. I thought I had put the cross in my pocket, but must have left it on the seat, and I discovered my loss later to my horror and shame.

That cross was a replica of the Canterbury Cross and a generous gift at the time I became a bishop. I've often held that cross for strength at difficult times. It was not its monetary value which caused it to mean so much to me but the fact that it had travelled with me throughout my episcopal ministry.

Three weeks went by. A final call to London Transport Lost Property revealed that they thought they had a necklace which answered my description. I did not mind what they called it. It was an unexpected blessing to receive it back again, especially as there was no record of who had found it. I did at least manage to express gratitude when talking about random acts of kindness on *Thought for the Day*. When we are blessed, we find believing that the world is good and that creation is the work of a loving God to be just a little easier. And the greatest blessings sometimes seem to come unexpectedly.

God of the unexpected, keep us alert to your presence in our encounters, so that we may be a blessing to others as you are a blessing to us. Amen.

14

Papua New Guinea 1: Popondetta

Matthew 16.24, 25

Popondetta is the capital of Oro (Northern Province) in Papua New Guinea. The Anglican cathedral is situated in the heart of the town. It is a simple, yet dignified, structure, more memorable than many other grander cathedrals. For the Cathedral of the Resurrection has a nave with no walls. There are simply pillars to keep the roof in place. This is a tribute to the climate, of course, and the cheapest form of air conditioning. The sanctuary is spacious, well-appointed and attractive. Those driving past on the road can scarcely miss seeing worship going on. They notice the great altar even when the church is empty. As it is, the cathedral never seems to be empty. There's always someone sitting, praying or resting there in the presence of God.

The contrast between the cathedral at Popondetta and the closed or even locked doors of so many churches in England has stayed with me over the years. Norwich Cathedral's great west doors are frequently left open during the summer months and during worship so that passers-by and visitors may observe and, if they wish, be drawn in to what's going on inside. At the Cathedral of the Resurrection at Popondetta, 'public' worship is exactly that. The absence of walls seems symbolic, too, of a church open to the society in which it is set, a church of service willing to receive from the world around it. It may be no accident that the small Anglican church in Papua New Guinea has taken the lead throughout the country in providing medical care and ministry for those affected by HIV/AIDS.

In August 2015, 12 pilgrims left Norwich for Papua New Guinea, meeting up with others from Rockhampton in Australia and Waiapu in New Zealand. All three dioceses have strong links with Papua New Guinea. Our visit coincided with the commemoration on 2 September of the martyrs of Papua New Guinea, a date observed throughout the Anglican Communion. The story behind it deserves to be better known.

The Bishop of Popondetta, Lindsley Ihove, was surprised and humbled that a group of English, Australian and New Zealand Anglicans should come on pilgrimage to Papua New Guinea and Popondetta in particular. Both he and other Anglicans locally were very familiar with pilgrimage as a concept and many of them dreamed of the possibility of being pilgrims one day to the Holy Land or to Canterbury. To discover that they themselves lived in a country so touched by the presence of God through martyrdom and sacrifice that others would travel thousands of miles to be with them was an unexpected encouragement. It happened because they remember their martyrs so well.

During the Second World War, Japanese forces advanced through South East Asia, capturing Rabaul, the capital of New Britain off the east coast of Papua New Guinea on 23 January 1942. A week later the bishop, Philip Strong, broadcast a radio message to his clergy and missionaries. He said:

> As far as I know you are all at your posts,
> and I am very glad and thankful about this.
> We must endeavour to carry on our work in
> all circumstances, no matter what the cost
> may ultimately be to any of us individually.
> God expects this of us. The Universal
> Church expects it. The people whom we
> serve expect it of us. Our own consciences
> expect it of us. We could never hold up

our faces again if, for our own safety, we all forsook him and fled.

In the event it was several months before Japanese forces reached the Popondetta area, from where they sought to advance to take Port Moresby, the capital. During August 1942, four priests, two mission sisters, two mission teachers, a lay worker and two Papuan evangelists were all killed by the Japanese forces or by local Papuans who were aiding the invaders.

The Martyrs Memorial School, about 15 kilometres from Popondetta itself, was founded in 1948. It commemorates those who had died for their faith only six years earlier. Its 700 pupils, most of whom board, know the story of the martyrs well. The fact that most of the missionaries originally came from Australia and England but stayed with the local people when their lives were in danger has been remembered and treasured. Had they deserted their posts it's unlikely the Anglican Church would have grown as it has done in more recent years. The same applies to other churches, which also have their martyrs from this period. In the last two generations, Papua New Guinea has become an overwhelmingly Christian country with one of the highest church-going rates in the world. The blood of the martyrs is indeed the seed of the Church.

At Jegarata, a few kilometres from Popondetta, two missionary sisters, May Hayman (a nurse) and Mavis Parkinson (a teacher), were bayoneted. Near that site in 2015 I saw for the first time a simple memorial close to where they were killed. A white altar with an inscription stands in a clearing to commemorate the two women, whose bodies have since been interred elsewhere.

Few people visit this remote location, yet fresh flowers stood upon the altar and the garden surrounding it is beautifully tended. Our visit was impromptu and unexpected. It was evident that local people cared deeply for that shrine. They appeared immediately to join us. It's a memorial which does not rate a mention in any guidebook, but what struck me was how tenderly and devotedly it was preserved and honoured by very poor local Christians.

What adds to the poignancy is that May Hayman was newly engaged to the Revd Vivian Redlich, a mission priest from England, who had been killed a few days earlier, though it's very unlikely that she would have known this. Vivian was urged by local people to flee since they knew he and other missionaries would be targeted. A final letter to his father in England just before he was killed survives, in which he says, 'No news of May and I am cut off from contacting her ... I am trying to stick, whatever happens. If I don't come out of it, just rest content that I have tried to do my job faithfully.'

There are no walls in the cathedral at Popondetta. There seems also to be a seamless connection between the life of the Church in Papua New Guinea today and the witness of the martyrs not so very many years ago. It's a place open to God.

> *Lord, you endowed the martyrs of Papua New*
> *Guinea with a steadfast spirit when their*
> *lives were threatened; give us the resolution to*
> *stay constant in our loyalty to you whatever*
> *challenges we face. Amen.*

15

Shaw's Corner,
Ayot St Lawrence

2 Timothy 1.8–14

Ayot St Lawrence is a small village just five miles from Welwyn Garden City in Hertfordshire. It has two main claims to fame. In 1777, Sir Lionel Lyde, living in the newly constructed Ayot House, found that the existing parish church inhibited his view. So he began the process of demolition. It's said that when the bishop heard of it, the destruction was halted, so a picturesque ecclesiastical ruin remains to this very day. Sir Lionel did build a new church, completed in 1778, designed in a neo-classical style. An English parish church in the form of a Greek temple in the Hertfordshire countryside seems eccentric to this day.

Ayot St Lawrence's second claim to fame is that George Bernard Shaw lived there for over 40 years. The Church of England built a new rectory in Ayot in 1902. It's a substantial Arts and Crafts house, but by 1906 it was already being offered, fully furnished, for rent. The parish was not large enough to warrant a resident incumbent. It drew Shaw's interest, not least because there is a tombstone in the churchyard to 'Mary Anne South. Born 1825. Died 1895', to which is added 'her time was short'.

Shaw decided that Ayot St Lawrence lent itself to longevity. He and his wife Charlotte eventually bought the house in 1920. After Charlotte died in 1943, Shaw pledged the house to the National Trust, dying himself in 1950. It isn't the architecture that makes it an obvious National Trust property, but the distinguished former occupant, whose hats, sticks, pens and furnishings remain much as they were at the time of his death.

Harold Nicolson, the diplomat and author, urged the National Trust not to accept the gift of Shaw's Corner. He predicted that Shaw would be completely forgotten 50 years after his death. While Shaw's reputation has been as uncertain in death as in life, the past decade has seen a good many revivals of his plays. Nicolson was wrong.

Living near Shaw's Corner for several years, we took a good many visitors there. Shaw was treated with a good deal of disdain by those who taught me about

English literature, but it was perhaps not his dramatic writings that alienated people so much as the man himself. Although he refused a knighthood and even the Order of Merit, this appeared to be the consequence of conceit rather than a deep humility. Once a Fabian and a borough councillor in London, Shaw claimed that both sides in the First World War were morally culpable, and this offended many, even in the Labour Party, at the time.

Later, Shaw promoted eugenics, the science of improving the human race by controlling parentage, discouraging reproduction by those of low intelligence or with genetic defects. To add to his notoriety, Shaw also expressed admiration at different times for Lenin, Mussolini and Hitler, believing that, in general, human beings were so flawed in their judgement that they needed a dictatorship. Shaw's dismissal of organized religion, his opposition to vaccination (he thought it was a cheap way for the government to avoid giving the poor good housing) and his promotion of alphabet reform made him unpopular with a wide range of people. I remember approaching my first visit to Shaw's Corner with both distaste and curiosity.

It was seeing Shaw's personal relics, and recognizing his fascination with the story of Joan of Arc, as well as learning more about his evolving under-standing of religion, that gradually caused me to change my mind. In the dining room at this time, his fountain pen and propelling pencil could be found alongside the old-fashioned steel-rimmed spectacles he wore in his final years. There was a gold coin minted in the reign of Charles VII of France during the lifetime of Joan of Arc, and acquired, presumably, as a result of his writing of *Saint Joan*.

In the garden was a writing hut, a tiny room meas-uring only 64 square feet but able to be rotated so that it could follow the light of the sun. It is small and unpretentious. I discovered, too, that Shaw had both his and Charlotte's ashes scattered in the gar-den around the statue of St Joan, to whom he had such devotion.

In his youth, Shaw had discarded the Protestant Christianity of the Church of Ireland in which he was brought up. He declared himself an atheist. But, later in life, he began to expound a more religious view of the world, believing in a life force behind the universe, a higher purpose, a great will, engaged in a continual struggle to produce something higher and more noble than the present state of the world suggests. Shaw described religious people as those who conceive themselves to be the instrument of this higher purpose in the universe, and who make it their business and joy to do the work of that great will and to identify themselves with it.

Shaw never seemed to comprehend that this life force, whom Christians call God, could or would inaugurate a better world through his own will and gift. Or if he did grasp the concept, he did not believe human beings would accept it. This appears to be the concluding message of his play about St Joan.

In the final scene of *Saint Joan*, she is cleared of heresy 25 years after her death. A messenger from the twentieth century arrives with news that she has been canonized by the Catholic Church. Joan herself then appears and testifies that saints can work miracles. She asks if she can be resurrected. Her defenders leave her one by one. The play ends with Joan realizing, with a mixture of despair and regret, that humankind never readily accepts saints. They speak of another world, and a higher purpose to which frail humanity is attracted but from which it then shrinks. St Joan says: 'O God that madest this beautiful earth, when will it be ready to accept thy saints? How long, O Lord, how long?'

At Shaw's Corner I sensed that *Saint Joan* may have meant more to Shaw than any of his other plays. It was not a play written by an atheist, but by someone who saw how sanctity both attracts and repels human beings at one and the same time.

> *God our Father, as we pray 'your will be done on earth as it is in heaven', may we perceive your holiness in those who seek to follow your call without reserve after the pattern of your Son Jesus Christ. Amen.*

16

Norwich Cathedral 1:
The Bishop's Chair

Exodus 25.17-22

Norwich is the only cathedral north of the Alps which has retained the bishop's chair in its elevated position at the east end of the apse above the high altar. Following the pattern of a Roman basilica, it is the chair of a teacher and leader of the community around whom clergy and people gather. Below the simple chair are the remains of stones from the ancient bishop's throne at North Elmham, the site of the see prior to its brief eleventh-century move to Thetford before Norwich established itself as the dominant centre of East Anglia.

One of the strange experiences of sitting on a throne so high and lifted up is that it creates a sense of exposure. The steps are narrow, so it is also precarious. I hadn't realized just how vulnerable and fragile someone sitting on a throne can feel. Perhaps this is why bishops have thrones. Those who are meant to be servants of the people of God are put in an exposed position to remind them of their need of grace.

I am not sure that's how some of my predecessors felt, especially those like Henry Despenser in the fourteenth century, who led armies and wore armour as often as donning vestments. But in an age like our own when (despite bishops sitting in the House of Lords) the Church in England wields relatively little secular power, the irony of this elevated position must surely be obvious to any bishop with the least degree of sensibility.

It is the bishop's chair – 'cathedra' in Latin – which makes a church a cathedral, rather than the grandeur of the building. The 'cathedra' grounds the bishop's ministry in a particular location. Even when empty, the chair is a symbol of the bishop's pastoral care for all, as well as a visible reminder of authority and order in God's Church.

The bishop's chair in every cathedral is empty nearly all the time. Being unoccupied does not rob it of significance. Perhaps my nonconformist childhood meant that the episcopal throne in Norwich has always prompted me to think of the empty mercy-seat in the tradition of the Salvation Army. Salvationists usually eschew symbols, but the mercy-seat has a very powerful presence in their places of worship, which are usually called citadels. The mercy-seat is a place of prayer where those responding to the call of Christ are received. While it can be used by anyone who feels the need, it is hallowed not by splendour (mercy-seats are plain) but by being the place where lives are given to Christ and he comes to those who trust him.

The mercy-seat on the Ark of the Covenant (Leviticus 16.2) was the place of God's presence. From there God's judgement was dispensed and his mercy bestowed. Since the God of Israel was not himself represented in wood or stone, the empty mercy-seat with the two cherubim protecting it at each end was testimony to the universal judgement and mercy of God. It was both a place for God and a reminder that every place was God's place. No bishop can minister without needing God's mercy, for episcopal consecration has a particular capacity for exposing human and spiritual weakness. The elevated eastern throne in Norwich is, above all, a mercy-seat.

The Norwich throne offers another theological lesson. When seated there, the bishop can look beyond the pulpitum (the great stone screen which separates the nave from the presbytery) and if the great west doors are open, he can see directly into The Close and the street beyond, at least 400 feet distant. From the episcopal throne the bishop is thus invited by the architecture to focus on the world outside. Was this precisely what those who built Norwich Cathedral more than nine centuries earlier intended? Was it an accidental alignment? I doubt it. At my enthronement I sensed God was teaching me something at the very moment I was commissioned for a new ministry.

Perhaps the greatest enthronement sermon preached in the twentieth century was given by Michael Ramsey in Canterbury Cathedral in June 1961. He took as his text, 'There went with him a band of men whose hearts God had touched' (1 Samuel 10.26). He spoke of the way in which a king was chosen for the first time in Israel. He described it as 'a task beyond all human strength' and commented that many were sure to be hostile and estranged. 'But he was not alone, there went with him a band of men who had felt the touch of God. It made all the difference.'

Ramsey went on to remind everyone that at their enthronement a bishop was put in the seat of a ruler 'for in Christ's name he will rule in the Church of

God, not indeed as in lording over it, but as serv-
ing it'. But he also recognized it was 'the putting
of a man into the chair of a teacher', for he understood that a bishop is a teacher of God's truth.
Ramsey went on to invite others to come with him
in a shared Christian profession. 'Come with me, in
the service of Christ: Come with me, we need one
another.'

It was a different age. Moving though that sermon
still is even today, the invitation was to come and
share. It could hardly be criticized for not being
scriptural since 'come, follow me' is so central to the
gospel, but it was an invitation to come and share the
Christian journey, to come and join us. When I sat
on the bishop's cathedra for the first time in Norwich
I was conscious that the perspective was not intended
to draw others to come to me but was an invitation
for me to go to them. For Christ commands us to 'go
forth into all the world'. The imperative in Norwich's
ancient throne, where no one but the bishop ever sits,
was not to stay there but to move out.

> *God of mercy, your Son was lifted high on the*
> *Cross to draw all people to himself. Raise us*
> *up in your presence, so that we may have a*
> *true perspective on the world you love so much*
> *and that we are called to serve. Amen.*

17

Norwich Cathedral 2:
St Luke's Chapel

Luke 4.18

Every Friday the early morning and lunchtime Eucharists in Norwich Cathedral are celebrated in St Luke's Chapel. This is where the Despenser Retable is sited, a remarkable and vivid altarpiece dating from the late fourteenth century. Henry Despenser was one of the most feared and fearsome bishops of Norwich. He began his episcopal ministry at the early age of 30 in 1367 and served until his death nearly 40 years later. He was instrumental in putting down the Peasants' Revolt in 1381. The Retable is believed to have been commissioned by him shortly afterwards in thanksgiving for the restoration of good order. Its delicate beauty is a vivid contrast to the violence and suppression which it commemorates. A notice at the entrance to the chapel describes the provenance of this fine altarpiece. Over the years I have received a number of letters from people who are disturbed by the cause for which it was commissioned. They seem to think the art itself is degenerate, sullied by the violence of the man who commissioned it.

The themes of the Retable are intriguing in the light of such questions. Jesus, himself subject to the secular power of his own time, has been condemned to death by crucifixion. The first two of the five panels of the Retable show Jesus being flogged and then carrying his cross to Golgotha. The central panel depicts the crucifixion itself. The resurrection and the ascension of Christ are pictured in the final panels. Both are illustrated in a very literal manner. The message is that Jesus is vindicated. He has passed to heavenly glory, but his authority has not vanished. It is now exercised by his Church. Hence the reason why this art was designed to be displayed at the back of an altar. Its message may well have been more obvious to people six centuries ago than it is now. If the power of Christ had transferred to his Church and those in authority within it, the message to those who viewed the painting was 'be obedient'.

The painting would have seemed traditional even in its own time. Its conservative style was like everything else we know about Henry Despenser. He had little regard for novelty of any sort. He was

100

uncompromising in his response to the protests of Lollards against the superabundance of images in the life of the Church. He showed no mercy to those early reformers. Included in the surrounds of the panels are the coats of arms of Norwich and Norfolk families who supported the bishop in maintaining order. The close connection between Church and State is presented unabashed. They were part of the same divine economy. Despenser saw himself as the King's good and faithful servant. We know Richard II visited Norwich with his wife, Anne of Bohemia. It is quite possible that the unveiling of the Retable took place during that visit, even though we have no direct record of the event. In recent times the Retable left the cathedral for an exhibition entitled *Masterpieces* at the Sainsbury Centre at the University of East Anglia, a testimony to its place in the history of art.

Today we interpret the painting very differently. When we read the Gospels we see how Jesus was the victim of the religious and secular powers of his own day. He is crucified for speaking the truth. His resurrection is God's vindication of him, a sign that God, who blesses the poor, is on the side of the peasants more than the powerful. I doubt Bishop Despenser would have envisaged anyone interpreting his painting this way. Yet we do. And it is not fanciful to see the painting in the light of this understanding of the gospel.

The message of great art can never be controlled by those who commission it. It cannot even be possessed or owned by the artist. A work of art takes on a life of its own. This reflects something of the character of all creative activity. Art can be subversive and dangerous to those who want to be in power and control, even when they themselves have commissioned it.

At the Reformation the Despenser Retable was saved by being upturned and used as a table. Whether this was simply to meet a practical need or a deliberate means of preserving the painting we do not know. It survived unnoticed for three centuries until in 1847 someone took a look underneath and realized what a treasure it was. It returned to the cathedral and, fully restored, has been in St Luke's Chapel ever since.

Since 2015 St Luke's Chapel has also been home to a Chrismatory, hanging from the ceiling just above the font and containing the holy oils (in prodigious quantities). The Chrismatory was sited here because of the chapel's dedication to St Luke the physician and his association with the healing ministry.

To have the holy oils so visibly on display in the cathedral church helps to fulfil the vocation of the cathedral to be a place of daily sacramental life and teaching. To see the oils adjacent to the Despenser Retable suggests another interpretation. A painting which was once regarded as a sign of sacerdotal and secular power is now seen to tell the story of Jesus Christ healing the wounds of humanity through his suffering and death. In his resurrection and ascension Jesus does not eschew the role of the suffering servant but fulfils it. When we are anointed, whether at baptism or confirmation, in sickness or even near death, the sign of the cross is used with holy oil, a reminder that Christ eases our way into his kingdom through the gift of his life to us. In their proximity, the Despenser Retable and the holy oils speak now of a gentle saviour, recognized in his self-emptying – a power which comes through weakness and self-offering. The Retable has not changed. Nor has God. But our apprehension of what he tries to teach us has altered, though it is hard not to wonder what else ought to be obvious that we miss.

> *Anoint us, Lord, with your spirit of self-offering, so that we may follow you to the Cross and find there the source of new life. Amen.*

18

Norwich Cathedral 3:
The Hostry and Refectory

1 John 1.5–7

In 1968 Norman Hook was coming to the end of almost two decades as Dean of Norwich. When he arrived in 1952, the fabric of Norwich Cathedral was in a poor state. The great church had largely escaped the destruction of the so-called Baedeker air raids in the Second World War, which caused Norwich and other cathedral cities to suffer. This was due not least to a small army of volunteers who were vigilant in putting out the fires caused by incendiary bombs. War damage to the cathedral was thus limited, but routine maintenance had been at a very low level in wartime. By the time of Norman Hook's retirement, a vast amount of restoration work had been completed. In the 1960s, Norwich Cathedral, like many others, began to show signs of renewed spiritual and community life. Just 12 months before he retired, Dean Hook pondered the future in an address to the General Chapter. He said he had been looking into his crystal ball. (I trust he was speaking figuratively.) He saw two things:

> First, I can see the ruined Refectory restored, providing a hall big enough to house a diocesan synod. I can see it functioning as an eating place – where parties and groups visiting the cathedral can have a meal. Second, hard by the Refectory on the site of the ancient guest house I can see a splendid church house, with rooms where educational work can be done, rooms where people can meet socially, rooms which can house such things as a religious enquiry centre ...

Forty-two years after the then Dean of Norwich said these words, the Queen came to open a range of buildings which fulfilled those ambitions remarkably precisely, and formed the largest extension to any English cathedral since the Reformation. What added to their significance was that the new buildings fulfilled in modern form many of the functions of their medieval predecessors upon whose foundations the new buildings were raised up.

In the early nineteenth century no one really knew what cathedrals were for. They were sleeping giants.

At one stage there was even a serious proposal that Norwich Cathedral should be knocked down and all the stones shipped to Great Yarmouth as building material. It would have given a different character to the Great Yarmouth sea front, but the very idea serves as a reminder that cathedrals were not always seen as centres of vigorous Christian life, worship and service.

The refectory used by the monks of Norwich before the Reformation was the largest in Europe. It ran along the southern range of the cloisters. The western range contained the hostry, where monks and townspeople met each other to do business. It was where people were welcomed initially to the monastic community, and given hospitality, as the term 'hostry' implies. It took almost ten years to raise all the money needed for the modern recreation of these two buildings, both designed by Sir Michael Hopkins. At the northern end of the refectory, which provides a restaurant open to everyone, there is also a new reading room and other facilities for the substantial cathedral library. By some miracle, the arch leading into the ancient hostry had survived and is now an integral part of the modern building, which, like so many of Michael Hopkins's buildings, has a great deal of glass, ensuring the rooms are flooded with light. A new song school for the choirs, education rooms, a conference room and an exhibition hall make up the rest of the hostry. It connects to the cathedral as it originally did through the old locutory, a place of conversation for the monks of long ago.

I was showing an American visitor the hostry for the first time just prior to the official opening. He found the use of space and light inspirational, but when he attempted to describe his delight, he said, 'I can't find the right words.' He didn't need to find them. That was the point. Cathedrals have become more important, better appreciated and more loved for their inspirational spaces at a time when our society has begun to lose its trust in words. Whether words come from a political platform, a pulpit, a pamphlet or even via the internet, we don't always give them much authority. It is partly because there are too many of them. We are not always sure which words we can trust. In the days of fake news and a barrage of opinions via social media, it is not surprising if some of us need another language.

T. S. Eliot reflected on the overload of words on our minds and spirits 80 years ago. In his work *Choruses from 'The Rock'* he wrote:

> The endless cycle of idea and action
> Endless invention, endless experiment

Brings knowledge of motion, but not of
stillness;
Knowledge of speech, but not of silence;
Knowledge of words, and ignorance of
the Word.

Then Eliot asks a question:

Where is the wisdom we have lost in
knowledge?
Where is the knowledge we have lost in
information?

Long before the age of the internet, Eliot argued
that information overload does not nurture knowledge, let alone wisdom. But he was no cynic. Eliot
had a high doctrine of the creativity of the human
person. He celebrated our God-given instinct to
build sacred places. He recognized that our religious buildings are not simply utilitarian. Human
ambitions, dreams and our aspirations to the divine
are all expressed through them. A later section of
Choruses from 'The Rock' captures the aspiration that
lay behind the building of the extension to Norwich
Cathedral in our own age.

Now you shall see the Temple completed:
After much striving, after many obstacles;

For the work of creation is never without
    travail;
The formed stone, the visible crucifix,
The dressed altar, the lifting light,

Light

Light

The visible reminder of Invisible Light.

It was the blaze of light and the expansiveness of the hostry which rendered that early visitor unusually speechless. Jesus Christ is light of light. The spaciousness of Norwich Cathedral and its hostry and refectory speaks of a roomy God, one who enlarges us and expands our vision of him. They are functional spaces, yet they also allow us to glimpse the light of him who is beyond seeing, beyond describing, the Word of God whom no words can explain: Jesus Christ. Eliot's final section of *Choruses from 'The Rock'* leads us into praise and worship.

We see the light but see not whence it
    comes.
O Light Invisible, we glorify thee!

19

Devil's Island, French Guiana

Matthew 25.34–40

Not many places are beautiful and chilling at the same time. But three small volcanic islands a few miles off the coast of French Guiana, Les Iles du Salut, were home to almost 80,000 French prisoners for one hundred years until the early 1950s. Their name (Salvation Islands) seems ironic in the circumstances. Ile Royale, the largest island, was the reception point where the general population of the penal colony lived. Ile Saint-Joseph was for the most notorious criminals, often kept in solitary confinement. Ile Diable (Devil's Island), the smallest island, was for political prisoners. Nowadays no one lives on Devil's Island and the jungle has almost reclaimed it, so it looks like an ecological haven. Captain Alfred Dreyfus, its most famous prisoner, was marooned there from 1895 to 1899. The agonies of past prisoners means that the atmosphere everywhere is heavy, and the humidity adds a suffocating blanket.

Many buildings survive from the penal period on Ile Royale, even if in a ruined state. The infirmary, the commandant's house, the chapel: each is a gaunt reminder of a century of suffering. There is a children's cemetery, the graves being those of the children of the prison officers and staff, for tropical disease did not claim prisoners alone. But there are no graves for the thousands of prisoners. They were thrown into the shark-infested waters that surround the islands. The combination of natural beauty and inhumanity is disturbing. Nowadays there is a hotel on Ile Royale, but it must require a curious insensitivity to history and atmosphere to enjoy a vacation in such a place.

While the name of Alfred Dreyfus is still remembered, the details of his harrowing story are less well known.

In September 1894 Marie Bastian, a cleaner in the German embassy in Paris, found a memorandum (in a wastepaper basket) which contained some low-grade military secrets. She passed it to French military intelligence. It was of little value, but proved there was a spy in the French military who was in the pay of the Germans.

Three weeks later an ambitious and patriotic young officer, Alfred Dreyfus, was arrested and accused of being its author. When he was court-martialled, a unanimous guilty verdict was returned. Dreyfus was of Jewish origin, married with two young children. He came from a prosperous family and had a large private income. Originally from Alsace, he had a vehement dislike of Germans. Neither a need for money nor questionable loyalties made him a likely spy. He believed in a France that proclaimed justice and fraternity. Somehow, even on Devil's Island, he managed to hold on to this belief.

Dreyfus arrived there after a lengthy degradation ceremony in Paris in January 1895. He was paraded before a crowd of 20,000, who shouted, 'Death to Judas, death to the Jew.'

On Devil's Island Dreyfus succumbed to tropical fevers and lost weight rapidly because of the rancid meat he was given to eat. The humidity meant that his clothes never dried out. With no one willing to speak to him, he almost lost the power of speech. A palisade was built around him, which meant he could only see the sky. It was probably expected that he would die. Somehow he didn't. One of the most remarkable things about Alfred Dreyfus was that he survived. What he didn't know on Devil's Island was that he had become the most famous man in France. Everyone spoke about the Dreyfus Affair.

Handwriting experts said that Dreyfus could not have written the memorandum. Further investigations suggested he knew nothing of some of the things mentioned in the original note. But two things told against him. One was that at his trial he spoke for six hours and did not seem to betray any emotion, believing that the facts spoke for themselves. His judges thought a loyal Frenchman would shout and scream, but Dreyfus had faith in French military justice. As well as this, anti-Semitism was virulent in the military.

Dreyfus had been on Devil's Island for two years when the real spy in the case, Walsin Aesterhazy, was identified by a brilliant young intelligence officer, Georges Picquart. Picquart thought he would only have to show his superiors the facts and they would release Dreyfus. But the army organized a military trial for Aesterhazy which exonerated him. This caused the Dreyfus Affair to become national news. Émile Zola's open letter to the President on the subject – '*J'accuse*' – accused virtually everyone in the senior military and the press of spreading false rumours and lies, and of conspiring to cover up a miscarriage of justice. He appealed for an explosion of truth.

113

Violence erupted in Paris, where Jewish shops were looted. Zola himself was put on trial. Eight thousand people congregated outside Zola's courtroom, scarcely worried whether Dreyfus was guilty or not. To recognize his innocence would weaken the army and shatter the honour of France.

Zola was found guilty of libel but escaped to England. Eventually, in June 1899, the French Supreme Court referred Dreyfus's case back to the military court, and ordered that he should return from Devil's Island. Any anticipation of a triumphant vindication was mistaken. The military court again convicted Dreyfus of treason but 'with extenuating circumstances' and sentenced him to ten years' imprisonment and further degradation. The President of the Republic intervened. He raised with Dreyfus the possibility of a pardon. If Dreyfus accepted guilt he would then be released. Exhausted, and having been away from his family for too long, Dreyfus accepted the offer. Many of his supporters were frustrated by his admission. Some spurned Dreyfus himself. By now, public opinion was longing for civil peace and harmony. Dreyfus was finally declared innocent in 1906.

Throughout this time his wife Lucie and his children remained totally loyal to Dreyfus, despite the terrible deprivations they suffered. When in solitary confinement, Dreyfus lived for Lucie's letters, which always reiterated the same values of courage, love and patience.

During the First World War Dreyfus was mobilized, even though he had reached the age of 55, and revelled in the chance to serve his country. After his death in 1935, the Vichy Regime in France brought fresh persecution of Jews. Lucie and Alfred's son Pierre left for America. Lucie changed her name to protect herself from persecution and gained protection in a convent in Valence. Remarkably, she continued to write to family and friends about the goodness and beauty of the world, eventually dying in Paris after its liberation in December 1945.

Sometimes it's been said of Dreyfus that only a man with a dull and unimaginative spirit could have survived his ordeal. Perhaps, though, it was his faith in the reality of truth and justice that sustained him, coupled with knowing he was loved by Lucie and his children, even if the whole world turned against him. At Devil's Island I prayed for the many in our world who are unjustly imprisoned, hoping that they knew that someone loved them, and if denied human love, that they may know the love of God.

*Spirit of God, you proclaim release to captives
and promise that the oppressed will go free;
strengthen all victims of prejudice and
those unjustly imprisoned, so that they may
know liberation and the year of the Lord's
favour. Amen.*

20

Cana in Galilee

John 2.1–11

It is rather doubtful that modern Cana (Kefer-Kenna), about four miles north-east of Nazareth on the way to Tiberias, is actually Cana as mentioned in the Gospels. But it is where the Franciscans established themselves in 1641, relying on the testimony of earlier pilgrims that it was the site of Jesus' first miracle. A church built in the early part of the twentieth century sits above the remains of what seems to have been a first-century synagogue. Evidence of houses from the first century AD have also been found alongside what appears to be an ancient basilica.

Pilgrims come in large numbers to Cana, as do couples getting married. Modern Cana is not an especially prepossessing town and the church is unremarkable. In the surrounding shops, rather vinegary *vin ordinaire* is sold at inflated prices in honour of Christ's first miracle.

I had never developed much fondness for Cana and the little attraction it held for me diminished even further in 2015 when I was leading a pilgrimage group, mostly of curates from the Diocese of Norwich, and we were refused permission to celebrate an Anglican Eucharist in the church, despite it having been pre-arranged. A rather fierce nun said we were the wrong sort of Anglicans and could not use the vestments and sacred vessels, which were reserved for Roman Catholic clergy only. Given the hospitality elsewhere of the Franciscan Custody of the Holy Land, it was something of a surprise. We shook the dust from our feet and went to Mount Tabor instead, where a Franciscan friar went out of his way to give us a welcome and a venue for our Eucharist.

I look back on this experience now as something of a gift. It was a reminder of the sharp divisions which still exist in the Christian Church and which often find their focus at the Lord's Table. It drew me to ponder afresh the meaning of that first miracle of Jesus. It taught me, too, that it isn't simply beatific experiences in holy places that draw us to God; cantankerous nuns can do so as well.

In the story of the first miracle at Cana, Mary appeals to Jesus to prevent what is likely to be an embarrassing failure of hospitality on the part of the family (most likely relatives of Mary herself). My experience of a lack of hospitality in Cana made the very point of this miracle even more telling.

At this marriage in Cana, Jesus preached no sermon. He gave no speech. He didn't tell the couple how to get the best out of their relationship. As Austin Farrer once put it, 'He simply concerned himself with the supply of wine.'

Two thousand years ago, a wedding was a great community event at which the feasting went on for days. Even so, six stone water jars holding 20 to 30 gallons each would seem more than enough for a good party. Jesus was not sparing in his provision.

There have always been some rather severe Christians who find Christ's miracle at Cana uncongenial. Why did Jesus do something seemingly so trivial? Why would he encourage excess and self-indulgence on such a scale? If there was a temperance movement at the time, Jesus was certainly not part of it. Austin Farrer claimed it showed that Jesus came 'to take away the cold religion of duty and to bring a religion of delight'. He and his disciples were accused of not fasting – 'the Son of Man came eating and drinking' (Matthew 11.19). It is no surprise that a heavenly banquet is one of the favourite images Jesus uses of the kingdom of God.

What is striking about the miracle is that the guests at the wedding do not even know a miracle has taken place. Jesus meets the needs of the bridegroom and bride and their family, but the guests simply think it is a beautifully planned reception. When things go well we often fail to notice just how much thought for others, careful planning and hard work makes our enjoyment possible. In Christian ministry a huge amount of work undertaken by clergy and laity alike is unseen. Visits to the sick and dying, words of encouragement, advice and counsel to those who are troubled, the preparation of sermons and addresses, the time given to prayer: this is the hidden work of Christian ministers, ordained and lay, without which much that is public in the leadership of worship, mission and evangelism wouldn't happen at all.

Apart from Mary, there were just a few other people at Cana aware of what happened – not the guests, nor the host, but some of the servants. Those in the lowest place are the first to notice the transforming power of Jesus Christ. That's a pattern. Those to whom Jesus first revealed himself are generally of low social standing – shepherds, fishermen, tax collectors and here, domestic servants.

The wise men are something of an exception as intellectual seekers after truth. Most of the time it seems to be people who are not much on the lookout for the Messiah and are weighed down by the battle for human survival who are given special insight. Jesus is on the side of those who serve: 'the Son of Man did not come to be served, but to serve, and to give his life as a ransom for many' (Mark 10.45). In first-century Palestine you gained no kudos for being a servant; in an age of slavery, most had no choice. In our own time, everyone apparently wants to be of service to us. To be a 'service provider' is now a noble calling.

To be turned away at Cana was chastening. But it made us much more grateful for every other act of hospitality on that pilgrimage. Without that experience I doubt I'd have identified quite so fully with the crisis of hospitality that occurred when Jesus attended that wedding, and how he responded to it.

> *God of celebration, you gave us a foretaste of the new wine of your kingdom in Jesus Christ. May we follow the pattern of your hospitality as we anticipate the heavenly banquet for all humankind. Amen.*

21

Victoria Falls

Genesis 9.8–17

Following a reading of Genesis 9.8–17 about the promise of a rainbow, a preacher began his sermon with a series of questions. He asked why rainbows had inspired so many songs, and what lay beyond these great bows in the sky. He almost burst into song as he described rainbows first as visions and then illusions with nothing to hide.

His words seemed both intriguing and vaguely familiar. I had not placed them until he declared they were the reflections of a great contemporary philosopher called Kermit the Frog. He had been quoting 'The Rainbow Connection' from *The Muppet Movie*. This caused much mirth in the congregation.

The preacher then moved on but I became distracted in the sermon (bishops suffer from this tendency quite as much as other Christians). The mention of rainbows, illusions, visions and the fact they have 'nothing to hide' took me back to an unforgettable experience on my one and only visit to Victoria Falls. A walk through the rainforest there found me looking at rainbows dancing around my feet as well as observing the power and the beauty of the largest waterfall in the world. The sun, the spray, the vegetation, the power of the water, the colours of the refracted light: there was something elemental about it all. Although I realized the multicoloured rainbows above and around me were all the result of drops of water capturing the light of the sun, that scientific explanation didn't describe why I felt so connected with this rainbow experience. There was a Rainbow Connection, as Kermit the philosopher would put it. Or, perhaps, if we want a more established poet, then William Wordsworth comes to our aid.

My heart leaps up when I behold
   A rainbow in the sky:
So was it when my life began;
So it is now I am a man;
So be it when I shall grow old,
   Or let me die!
The Child is father of the Man;
And I could wish my days to be
Bound each to each by natural piety.

For Wordsworth, rainbows created a connection in his life from child to adult to old man, as well as a bond with nature. The rainbow as a symbol of a covenant ('bound each to each') is expressed clearly in the poem. Since the rainbow in Genesis is linked with God's promise never to destroy the earth by flooding again, it prompts 'a natural piety' in human beings.

Victoria Falls marks the boundary between Zimbabwe and Zambia. The Victoria Falls Bridge has border posts on the approaches to both ends – from the town of Victoria Falls in Zimbabwe and Livingstone in Zambia. The name of the latter town is a reminder that David Livingstone was reputedly the first European ever to see the falls. The boundary has sometimes been politically sensitive, most notably in 1965 when Southern Rhodesia unilaterally declared independence. It was not recognized by Zambia, the former Northern Rhodesia, let alone by the United Kingdom or much of the rest of the world. Military incursions, guerrilla warfare and the stationing of soldiers made this a sensitive demarcation. Border crossings became impossible. Even then, of course, rainbows recognized none of these boundaries. They enveloped warring peoples within their arc, a sign of the promise of better times.

In ancient traditions, the rainbow was usually a symbol of all that is life-giving. In Greek mythology, the rainbow marks the pathway of Iris, the messenger between the gods and humanity. Within Australian aboriginal myths, there is a rainbow serpent who is the creator of all life, giving fertility to the earth through abundance of rain. In the Bible, the rainbow is inseparable from the story of the Flood and Noah's Ark.

That story is often portrayed as one in which God's anger at the unfaithfulness of human beings leads him (almost) to destroy all living things. Perhaps, though, we should understand the whole story as one in which the covenant between God and Noah and his descendants is predicated not on demands for better behaviour but instead on God's gracious promise to set aside for ever the option of flooding the world. In ancient societies, putting down the bow used in war meant that arrows would no longer fly. In this story, God puts his bow, his rainbow, at rest in the sky: a sign of his pledge to love humankind no matter how atrociously human beings behave. 'I will establish my covenant with you, then never again shall all life be destroyed by the waters of a flood, and never again shall there be a flood to destroy the earth' (Genesis 9.11).

The rainbow has been appropriated by all sorts of good causes. It is a symbol for inclusivity, especially for the acceptance of LGBTI people. In the United States there was a time when the rainbow coalition encouraged multicultural participation in the electoral process. In Germany in the sixteenth century, the Peasants' Revolt used the rainbow as a symbol of their uprising against their feudal masters. Almost everywhere, the rainbow is a symbol of peace, acceptance and blessing.

No matter how powerful these traditions may be, I suspect that, in our culture, Judy Garland's song in *The Wizard of Oz* has even more purchase. Nowadays heard frequently at funerals, it promises a land of bliss at the end of the rainbow, where our dreams come true and troubles vanish. To go to Victoria Falls is to be vividly reminded of a much more profound and biblical understanding of the promise of the rainbow – the arc which embraces us all, the sign of the promise of God's mercy and unfailing kindness. And the fact that rainbows frequently have no discernible beginning or end, but grow and fade away, reflects the eternal life without beginning or end of God himself.

God of colour and Lord of light, as your rainbow covenant is a promise of unfailing kindness, so may we reflect your mercy by a spirit of unconditional acceptance of others. Amen.

22

Walsingham Abbey

Proverbs 9.10–12

The ruins of English medieval monasteries can be impressive, but I have sometimes found them spiritually desolate. Not so at Walsingham, though the story of the destruction of the Priory of Our Lady of Walsingham (it was never an abbey, despite its contemporary designation) was more venal and distressing than most.

When Richeldis, the lady of the local manor, received her vision in the eleventh century and felt compelled to create a replica of our Lord's home in Nazareth, pilgrims soon began to find their way to this remote settlement. Within a century, it had been entrusted to the care of Augustinian canons. They built their priory around the holy house.

The last prior of Walsingham was Richard Vowell. He was installed in 1514, following an episcopal visitation by the Bishop of Norwich, Richard Nix. The catalogue of scandalous living and financial corruption the bishop discovered would have been just what Thomas Cromwell's commissioners 20 years later would have been delighted to find, giving them good grounds for the dissolution of the priory. However, Richard Vowell presided over a considerable improvement in discipline and good order. He sought good relations with both the King and Thomas Cromwell, and Walsingham was one of the earliest religious houses to acknowledge the King's supremacy over the Church. Vowell was obsequious to the authorities, even when in 1537 his sub-prior and others were hanged outside the priory walls on flimsy charges. A year later, Prior Vowell assented to the destruction of the shrine and priory, the despoliation of the image of Our Lady and the confiscation of all the priory possessed. He pleaded his own cause and received a handsome pension – £100 per annum, which would have made him wealthy for the rest of his life.

For many years, the Anglican National Pilgrimage to Walsingham, which takes place on the spring bank holiday Monday, has used the grounds of Walsingham Abbey for its Mass, the afternoon sermon and, more recently, for Benediction too on the site of the original Holy House. Perhaps the restoration of worship and devotion has made this feel like a place at peace, one reconciled to its history where prayer may still come easily.

At the Anglican National Pilgrimage in May 2017, the Roman Catholic Bishop of East Anglia and I sat together on the dais, and we blessed matching icons which had been 'written' for both the modern Anglican and Roman Catholic shrines. The preacher was Fr Raniero Cantalamessa, the Preacher to the Papal Household and a Capuchin friar. Fr Cantalamessa preached about hope. In these surroundings where the severance between the Church of England and the Roman Catholic Church had found such violent expression, his words were powerful.

In November 2015 Fr Cantalamessa preached in Westminster Abbey at the inauguration of the General Synod. He spoke then of what Pope Francis calls 'reconciled diversities'; not the imposition of uniformity but one that seeks to 'fulfil Christ's heart's desire for unity'. He said that 'in many parts of the world people are killed and churches burned not because they are Catholic, or Anglican, or Pentecostals, but because they are Christians. In their eyes we are already one! Let us be one also in our eyes and in the eyes of God.'

How can this be when our structures and traditions are so different? Perhaps Walsingham offers a clue, since Anglicans, Roman Catholics, Methodists and the Orthodox of different traditions all live in close proximity, but also in a growing unity, though certainly not uniformity. Perhaps this is because religion at Walsingham is so visual and material, laced with image and symbol. It's a place where religion is not confined to the language of words.

Those without faith frequently assume the Christian religion exists entirely in our heads. What we believe does matter. But what we do matters as well. People pray when they are far from sure what they believe and to whom they are praying. *Lex orandi, lex credendi* – the law of praying is the law of believing – is frequently repeated in the Catholic tradition to describe the way in which our worship reflects our doctrine. But for many people it is prayer alone that comes first.

In 1982, when Pope John Paul II visited England, we seemed to reach a high-water mark of expectation in Anglican/Roman Catholic relationships. One Agreed Statement after another flowed from the Anglican/Roman Catholic International Commission. Perhaps our problem, though, was that we did not sufficiently heed *lex orandi, lex credendi*.

We appeared to think we would be able to negotiate our way to shared belief, rather than praying our way to the unity Jesus Christ wills for his Church. For all its many achievements, the Anglican/Roman Catholic International Commission seemed to be confined to our heads, whereas at Walsingham it is clear the Christian religion is about much more than that.

When, in 1966, Pope Paul VI took off his episcopal ring and gave it to the Archbishop of Canterbury, Michael Ramsey, it was a symbolic act which spoke volumes. The Pope would have been unlikely to give his ring to a lay person. Each succeeding Archbishop of Canterbury has worn that ring on visits to the Vatican.

Pope John Paul II, Pope Benedict XVI and Pope Francis have continued to give Archbishops of Canterbury episcopal insignia of one sort or another. Most recently, on 5 October 2016 at Vespers in San Gregorio al Cielo in Rome, Pope Francis gave Archbishop Justin Welby a replica of the crozier of Pope Gregory the Great. It was from San Gregorio in 597 that Pope Gregory sent Augustine (the first Archbishop of Canterbury) on his mission to England. The context, the nature of the gift and the recipient was not only symbolic of the search for unity but also a sign of a unity which already exists. At the same service, Archbishop Justin took off his pectoral cross, made of nails from the bombed ruins of Coventry Cathedral, and gave it to Pope Francis, who kissed it. The Pope said, 'Let us never tire of asking the Lord together and insistently for the gift of unity.'

Sometimes the Church seems to value words above symbols. Perhaps we are discovering through shared prayer and symbolic gestures what Fr Cantalamessa hoped for in his sermon to the General Synod. 'Let us be one also in our eyes and in the eyes of God.' Walsingham speaks the same language.

Give us the imagination, Lord, to grasp every opportunity to deepen our love for our brothers and sisters in Christ, and may we never tire of asking you insistently for the gift of unity. Amen.

23

Christ the King, Welwyn Garden City

John 18.33–37

I began my ordained ministry in the Church of Christ the Carpenter on the outskirts of Peterborough. I believe the dedication of the church may be unique. It was built in 1958 to serve a large council estate. I was told that the dedication was the idea of the wife of the then bishop, who thought it would create a sense of identity and connection with the artisan population.

Three and a half years later, I moved to Welwyn Garden City to a church dedicated to Christ the King. It seemed like a sort of elevation.

I had never compared the dedication of these two churches until I was interviewed at Church House in London for a job there. The Professor of Moral and Pastoral Theology in the University of Oxford, the late Peter Baelz, was one of the interviewers. He began with a question clearly designed to put me at my ease. 'I see you've served in two churches, one dedicated to Christ the Carpenter and the other to Christ the King. Does this suggest to you two models of the Church, and if so, what are they?' This is probably everyday conversation for a professor of theology. I'm not sure how I answered at the time, but it's a question that has stayed in my mind ever since.

A church dedicated to Christ the Carpenter suggests that God is a worker alongside us. He shares the labours, disappointments, joys and sorrows that are the stuff of human life. He is a God immersed in the life of the world. Christ the Carpenter plunges into our experience. In the dust and wood shavings of the carpenter's workshop the earthiness of human life is found.

If a church dedicated to Christ the Carpenter earths us in the divine realities of everyday life, then a church dedicated to Christ the King seems to suggest something quite different. If Christ is a king then he must preside over creation. His spiritual authority seems to come from the top down.

Both these churches were modern buildings. Christ the King was built in 1964, just six years later than my first church in Peterborough. Neither of them

135

could claim to be an architectural masterpiece, yet each has something that reflects its specific dedication. Christ the Carpenter in Peterborough possesses a west window over its entrance where the etchings on the glass depict carpenters' tools. They are reminders of Jesus working in an ordinary job alongside Joseph, living alongside us.

In my time at Christ the King there was a large crucifix above the main altar, but a Christus Rex was prominent in one of the side chapels. Such a crucifix has Jesus wearing a crown not of thorns but of majesty. He is also dressed in Eucharistic vestments on the cross. The Christus Rex symbolizes Christ the great high priest, reigning over creation from a cross which sinful humanity intended to be a tree of defeat but which became a tree of glory. The link between the Eucharist and Christ's sacrifice of himself for us is made clear too.

The different perspectives on Jesus Christ reflected in the two dedications of these churches are not mutually exclusive. Of the two, Christ the King is the humbler church. In 1964 it was built at the cost of £14,000, scarcely a king's ransom even then. A visiting preacher noted for his punctuality once arrived only just in time for the start of our service. He'd never been to Christ the King before, and explained, 'I drove past your church. I thought it was the fire station.'

A few weeks later, the Bishop of St Albans came for his first visit for a confirmation. As he got out of his car I could see that he was not overwhelmed by the beauty of the church either, though, being a bishop, he was too polite to say anything. Once he came inside, he turned to me and said, 'So it is a real church then?' I think I understood what he meant. He now saw the people busily preparing for the service and showing every sign, as did the church interior, that it was a place loved and cherished as a spiritual home, a place of encounter with the living God. In its design and external appearance it conveyed little of the kingship of Christ. But the church – as people rather than a building – reflected the glory of Christ, for they honoured him as king and saviour.

Jesus Christ is both carpenter and king. God is found in the ordinary and everyday, and in our common routines. But Jesus Christ is not only beneath our feet, he is also the Lord of glory. Even the grandest cathedral cannot give God enough glory.

There were some remarkable stories of lives changed by the grace of Christ in that very ordinary congregation at Christ the King. I think of the way in which a tragic accident and the forgiveness shown by the victim's family to the person who had unwittingly caused it became the source of all kinds of new life. I think of the daily care given by one member of the congregation to another who was disabled, ungrateful and often crotchety, a true sign of grace on the part of the carer, who received little thanks. I think too of the way in which engagement with the wider community led to the foundation of a residents' association and the eventual building of a community centre. The church may have been dedicated to Christ the King, but its life and ministry was grounded in the community that surrounded it. It was a ministry from below, and not only from the top down.

Sometimes our churches seem trivial, small-scale and lacking in impact compared with the enormity of the problems of the world. Yet even in places of little architectural beauty, where the liturgy and preaching may be no more than average, the gospel is heard and God's Spirit received just as much as in the mega-church with the celebrity speaker. At Christ the King in Welwyn Garden City, I realized that a very ordinary church – which had a priest and congregation marked by failures and mistakes – could be a community of transformation. There's nowhere like our churches. There's nowhere else proclaiming a faith in the Lord of glory who is also the God beneath our feet.

Lord Jesus Christ, carpenter of Nazareth and King of creation, open our eyes to your transforming presence in every place and circumstance. Amen.

24

St Peter's, Weedon:
The Ringing Chamber

1 Corinthians 13.1, 2

There are various locations that lay claim to be the centre of England, but Weedon in Northamptonshire has as good a claim as most. It was in 1803 at Weedon that a substantial range of buildings was established as a place of retreat for King George III if Napoleon invaded. There was never much prospect he would use them, but they later formed part of an extensive set of barracks where cavalrymen were trained.

Having spent the first years of my life a few yards from the Atlantic Ocean in Cornwall, it was a contrast as a teenager to live as far from the sea as it is possible to get in England. Weedon is surprising in other ways. The Watling Street (now the A5), the Grand Union Canal, the main railway line from Euston to the north, the River Nene and the main arterial A45 all converge there. A geography teacher at my secondary school once explained that where communication links converge, cities develop. It wasn't one of my more diplomatic moments when I pointed out to him, rather to his displeasure, that I lived where road, river, rail and canal links all crossed and there was only a village of 2,000 people. Weedon has grown a bit since then, but it is a long way from being a city.

The parish church, dedicated to St Peter, has a Norman tower, though the rest of it was rebuilt in the nineteenth century and is not architecturally distinguished. In my teenage years, when I could well have given up going to church, it was taking up the art of bell ringing that did as much as anything to keep me part of the church community. I cannot say it was devotion to the art of campanology that motivated me, but a number of the teenage girls in the village were learning to ring bells too. The ringing chamber (though it was in fact at floor level in the church) acted as a sort of informal youth club. Many and varied are the ways in which God keeps us in touch with the gospel.

Perhaps because the bells are rung at ground level and with the ringing area open to the nave of the church in Weedon, it always felt as if we were doing something for the church rather than being engaged in an unrelated activity in an elevated room.

Bell ringing is an activity that takes place in church but that is done entirely for those outside. The purpose of ringing is to call others, to announce that worship is about to take place, to celebrate the presence of God in the world by pealing out his praise. You don't always hear bells very clearly when sitting in church, whereas they may well be audible half a mile away or more. Over the years, I have come to appreciate the great variety to be found in bell ringers. I have seen old men with gnarled hands, the signs of a lifetime working the land, still pulling their sallies despite their bent backs and arthritic hips. I have seen young girls with delicate white hands standing on boxes with what seems like far too little strength to ring a bell at all. It is a mistaken notion that bell ringing has much to do with brute force. It's more to do with balance, sensitivity, feeling through your hands and muscles and indeed your whole body where a bell is on its wheel as it turns. It's about observing what your fellow ringers are doing, making allowances for them, and following them in your place.

In a ringing tower as a teenager I felt adults were treating me as an equal. It was a contrast to the tendency (common in my youth) for young people to perform in church and be applauded in a rather patronizing way. A good feature of bell ringing is that it is one of those few activities where teenagers can teach people who are a generation older. There is a little parable of the dignity of the Christian life here.

Bells are no new invention in our churches. Their connection with religion goes back a very long way. The people of Israel made bells of pure gold for the Tabernacle, the place of the presence of God. St Gregory, Bishop of Tours in the sixth century, mentions bells frequently in his writings about the church in France. We know there were bells in Ireland around the same time and their use probably spread to England by the seventh century, becoming more common a hundred years later. It was around that time that bells began to be blessed by a bishop. This seems to be because bells were to call people to worship. Their voice was charged with the invitation 'come, follow me'.

In more than 40 years since my ordination I have scarcely served anywhere with bells. When I was Bishop of St Germans in Cornwall I did sometimes ring at St Germans Church prior to a service, but I lived over 40 miles away in Truro. Norwich is one of only three cathedrals in England without a set of ringable bells. So I have become a very rusty bell ringer indeed. But I've never doubted that bells have qualities that should be reflected within the Christian life. A bell should send a consistent note. It shouldn't waver and change from day to day. It needs consistency of voice. A treble bell doesn't suddenly become a tenor or vice versa. God himself, his word and his love for us, has the virtue of constancy. While we blow hot and cold, God has spoken with a clear voice in Jesus Christ. No matter how inconsistent our response to him, his love for us is reliable. That's the good news.

Even the uninitiated can hear whether bells complement each other. It does not matter if they have no knowledge of ringing patterns such as rounds, changes or methods. In our congregations and church communities we have many different characters and voices. Sometimes they clash, for we are differently cast. But our corporate witness to Christ is most effective when we sound our different notes together in praising God. Christians sometimes seem slow to learn this lesson.

My initial attraction to the bell chamber at St Peter's, Weedon, had little to do with the attraction of the gospel and more with the galloping hormones of a teenage boy. But God uses our longings and desires and sometimes reshapes them creatively, perhaps without our being aware of it.

> *Give us, Lord, a clear voice to speak of you, the right tone to praise you, and a true sensitivity to those with whom we engage in the service of your Church and people. Amen.*

25

Butrint, Albania

James 1.2–4

Butrint lies in the far south-west of Albania. It's accessible from Sarande, nowadays a thriving coastal resort with a significant Greek population. Driving from Sarande to Butrint, concrete bunkers are visible alongside the road. They were used as lookout posts with gun emplacements during the Stalinist rule of Enver Hoxha, Albania's leader from 1944 until his death in 1985. During that period the country was almost entirely cut off from the rest of the Western world. It's estimated there were 750,000 concrete bunkers built in Albania during Hoxha's time – one for every four people in the country. Under Communist rule Albanians did not want for observation or oppression. Hoxha taught them to fear foreign invasion. In truth, there was little to attract other powers.

In 1967 this Muslim-majority country, the only one in Europe, was proclaimed an atheist state. Albania suffered what was probably the most systematic obliteration of religion – all religion – ever attempted in Europe. Hundreds of mosques were demolished. Some were turned into community halls. Ninety-five per cent of all church buildings were knocked down. The total removal of all religion and any memory of it was the sole aim and purpose of this policy. It didn't work. Faith went underground. While faith isn't dependent on shrines, once Albania tasted religious freedom again in 1990, mosques and churches were rebuilt.

It is strange to go to an ancient land denuded of historic churches, mosques, temples and shrines. Butrint is important because it is a witness to a different history in earlier centuries when the impulse to destroy was not so all-consuming. Civilizations and belief systems succeeded one another without obliterating what came before. The place survived because it was no longer home to any living community during the years of Communism, but its stones tell a story. A Greek colony was established there in the sixth century BC. It became a significant trading city, heavily fortified, with gates still standing today. In 167 BC when the Romans took over they had plenty of substantial buildings to inherit, and extended the original Greek theatre. The

147

Byzantines made Butrint an ecclesiastical centre. A baptistery and a basilica are still impressive. From a later period, there is a Venetian castle. While the Romans, the Byzantines and the Venetians all added to their own distinctive culture, they did not destroy but adapted what came before. Hoxha broke with that Albanian tradition.

At the end of the Second World War, Albanians were in a desperate state. They were an impoverished people in a devastated country. About 30,000 Albanian civilians had been killed in the conflict and many thousands were homeless. The Communist government, established in 1944, engaged in a house-building programme, nationalizing such industry, banking and transport infrastructure as still existed. State farms and cooperatives were set up. The 1950s saw growing links with China. Albania took China's side in quarrels with the Soviet Union. It withdrew from the Warsaw Pact. With Chairman Mao's death in 1976, China lost interest. It cancelled all its aid programmes to Albania, rendering it one of the most introverted countries in the world.

Enver Hoxha's proclamation of an atheist state in 1967 confirmed a policy that had been in place for much of the previous 20 years. Inspired by the Cultural Revolution in China, a new round of imprisonments and executions of religious believers began. After being beaten publicly in the square in front of his cathedral, the Roman Catholic Archbishop of Tirana, Ernest Coba, was sent to work on a collective farm. A Catholic priest, Fr Stephen Kurti, had been sentenced to 20 years imprisonment in 1945 on trumped-up charges of espionage. He was released in 1962, took up parish work again, and, after all churches were closed in 1967, went to work in a warehouse. For protesting about the destruction of a church building he was sentenced to internment in a corrective labour camp. Once there, he baptized a child secretly at the request of its mother. Fr Kurti was sentenced to death and executed in February 1972. He was one of many who suffered, but his story is better documented than others.

When I visited Albania a few years ago I realized that the persecution of religion had been going on during the early years of my ordained ministry and yet I knew very little about it. There was an attempt at that time to replace religious festivals with secular celebrations. Border Guard Day or the Festival of Electric Light didn't create much joy and delight in a country of such dour poverty. Even the names of children were controlled by the state. No saints' names were allowed. A dictionary of

3,000 acceptable names was published as recently as 1982.

The irony is that, from 1967, when it was declared that religion would be removed entirely from Albania, the fame of an Albanian nun began to grow throughout the world. Mother Teresa was born Agnes Gonxha Bojaxhiu in 1910 to Albanian parents living in Skopje, now in Macedonia. In 1928 she left to become a nun, the most famous religious sister of the twentieth century. Even the international airport in Tirana is now named after her.

In 1989, just before the fall of Communism, Mother Teresa visited Tirana. She was officially greeted by the Communist Foreign Minister and by the widow of Enver Hoxha. This was a typically surprising gesture on Mother Teresa's part. How was it that she would meet the wife of such a virulent destroyer of Christianity in her country? She even placed flowers on Enver Hoxha's grave.

Mother Teresa said, 'By blood, I am Albanian. By citizenship, an Indian. By faith, I am a Catholic nun. As to my calling, I belong to the world.'

The layers of archaeological ruins in Butrint are stunning. To see them in a country where there was such a determined attempt to remove the legacy of centuries of religious faith both in buildings and beliefs makes them the more valuable. Perhaps, however, the layers of belonging described in the words of an Albanian nun illustrate why faith and vocation are so hard to obliterate, and possess an astonishing durability.

> *God of eternity, when we are perplexed by*
> *persecution, indifference and unbelief, may*
> *we remember the durability of faith in you,*
> *and take delight in belonging to a company of*
> *believers found in every age. Amen.*

26

Papua New Guinea 2:
Kwima, Jimi Valley

Deuteronomy 28.3–6

My first visit to Papua New Guinea was in August 1991, to support Archbishop George Carey's first overseas visit to a province of the Anglican Communion. It celebrated the centenary of the arrival there of the first Anglican missionaries, Albert Maclaren from England and Copland King from Australia.

They met with no immediate success since Maclaren died before the end of 1891 and Copland King withdrew to Australia, returning later and slowly establishing a mission house in Dogura in the southeast of the country. A large Modawa tree at Dogura, which grew out of a corner post in the first bush chapel, is still vigorous today. It's regarded as a symbol of the growth of the Church.

I returned to Papua New Guinea in August 2015. The Diocese of Norwich has had a strong link with the Anglican Church there for more than 60 years. In 1946 a young priest, David Hand, who grew up in a Norfolk vicarage, offered himself for mission work in that country. He became the youngest bishop in the Anglican Communion in 1950 at the age of just 32. David Hand must be one of the last missionaries to have encountered peoples who had never previously met anyone from the outside world.

Until the 1950s, the Western Highlands of Papua were so remote that the wider world did not know that hundreds of thousands of people lived there. The area now forms part of the Diocese of Aipo Rongo. From Mount Hagen, the main urban centre and our base in 2015, we travelled more than six hours, mostly over very primitive tracks through a mountainous region of dense undergrowth to a village called Kwima in the Jimi Valley. Getting there was a tribute to our Toyota Landcruiser, which seemed to cope with almost any terrain. On arrival we were greeted by hundreds of people, some of whom had walked for several days from even more remote villages. The welcome ceremony was elaborate. It included men dressed as warriors, their faces painted black. Their wooden spears could have done a lot of damage if used in anger. Until

153

the gospel reached this area a couple of generations ago, the hostility between different groups, many of whom did not understand each other (there are over 800 languages in Papua New Guinea), often led to conflicts, deaths and even cannibalism.

We went to Kwima for the consecration of a new Anglican church, built by the people themselves but under expert guidance from an English priest, Fr Barrie Slatter, who, with his wife, had become greatly loved by the people of the Jimi Valley. Before ordination Barrie Slatter was a chartered surveyor. He discovered that many of the local men were quick learners in the arts of joinery, carpentry and construction. After all, they had been well versed in creating homes and shelters from whatever was to hand, and with nothing but the simplest tools.

St Alban's Church, Kwima, is easily the grandest building in the village. The congregation expects to spend hours there in worship on Sundays (and other days too). It is the central building in everyone's lives.

The people had built a hut for us to stay in. Seven of us slept on the floor in one of the rooms. As I lay there I realized I could not have begun to construct even the simplest shelter. Left to my own devices, and with a small plot of land in Kwima, I would be unable to feed and clothe myself, if deprived of money, shops and the infrastructure of a developed economy. My supposed intelligence and sophistication was put into perspective against the skills, capacity and ingenuity of the people among whom I was living.

The local bishop and I confirmed 200 young people at an evening service, all of them wearing gleaming white t-shirts for the occasion, indicating that Western influences can be felt even in the remotest parts. The sort of questions that we ask in our culture, such as 'Are you religious?' or 'Do you believe in God?', seemed entirely alien here. God was in the air people breathed, in the land they farmed, in the hymns they sang, in the sacraments they received, and in the community in which they lived. We read a passage from Deuteronomy 28 about the blessings which come from faithfulness to God.

Blessed shall you be in the city, and blessed shall you be in the field.
Blessed shall be the fruit of your womb, the fruit of your ground, and the fruit of your livestock, both the increase of your cattle and the issue of your flock.
Blessed shall be your basket and your kneading bowl.

155

> Blessed shall you be when you come in, and
> blessed shall you be when you go out.
>
> (Deuteronomy 28.3–6)

This scripture needed no interpretation for the
people of the Jimi Valley. It spoke directly to their
experience. The sense of God's blessing in their lives
was greater here than I have met almost anywhere
else. Perhaps the promise of blessing in the Mosaic
covenant may be more immediately recognizable to
people living within an agrarian economy. It is love
for God that motivates the people of Israel to keep
the law and remain faithful to the covenant. The first
command in Deuteronomy is the command to love
the Lord (6.5). In the Jimi Valley it was clear that
the people's great love for God came from knowing
he first loved them. That generated faithfulness and
a powerful sense of God's blessing.

In John's Gospel, Jesus seeks from his disciples a
depth of love mirroring that which the Lord claims
from Israel in Deuteronomy. Jesus even goes so far
as to tell his disciples that if they love him, they will
keep his commandments (John 14.15; 15.10).

In Kwima I admired the astonishing self-sufficiency
of the people. Even more evident was their love of
God and sense of God's blessing. A life close to the

land within communities of intimacy may create a profound receptivity to the gospel, just as in the Western world our distance from the land and the atomization of family and community life so easily closes our eyes and ears to the blessings of God's good news.

> *God of the meek and lowly in heart, enable us to understand that those who live most simply in our world possess the true wisdom that comes from knowing your blessing of land and people. Amen.*

27

Conques, France

Romans 12.1–5

I visited Conques in southern France almost by accident when spending a weekend in the region. The abbey church is a Romanesque masterpiece. The village is a popular resting place for pilgrims on their way to Santiago de Compostela. The church contains the relics of St Foy, known to the English as St Faith. I had long known of St Faith and that she was an early virgin martyr. I had worshipped in St Faith's Chapel in Westminster Abbey and preached at St Faith's, Crosby, on Merseyside (Archbishop Robert Runcie's home church).

At Conques I learned more of the story of St Faith. She is recorded in the *Martyrologium Hieronymianum* (Martyrology of Jerome), and probably died at Agen in Gaul in the late third century. Some claim that she was a victim of the Diocletian Persecution in 303. It's likely she was a young Christian martyred in the final years of the Roman Empire prior to Constantine's conversion. Beyond that, we know very little. At one stage she became confused with the three legendary sisters St Faith, St Hope and St Charity, whose mother was St Sophia – wisdom. Virtues became personified. Whether St Faith was roasted on a brazier before being beheaded (there was considerable competition among biographers when it came to recording grisly details of early saints' deaths) no one can say. But her faith caused her to be remembered and venerated, and that may also account for her name. Her relics were preserved. It is a deeply Christian instinct to remember with thanksgiving those whose faith has been vivid or whose deaths have been sacrificial, and to treasure their physical remains.

St Faith's relics remained in Agen until a monk from Conques stole them in 866. It is not a very edifying story, but they have remained in Conques ever since.

Within ten days of my unexpected visit to Conques, I made a pastoral visitation to Horsham St Faith in the Diocese of Norwich. The parish church there is dedicated to St Mary and St Andrew, but in the early thirteenth century there was a priory dedicated to St Faith. On this visit (for the church's patronal festival, which they keep on the feast of St Faith) I was able to tell the parishioners of my visit to Conques. It did seem a surprising coincidence, especially as, the previous year, two of the Norbertine fathers from Conques had visited Horsham St Faith for the same festival.

I also visited the priory behind the church. It has long been a private residence and contains the best mid-thirteenth-century wall paintings to be found anywhere in an English house. A very large depiction of the crucifixion survives to this day. It shows Mary and John gazing at Jesus, and high on the same wall a crowned figure, St Faith, is seen too. Beneath are a series of paintings showing why a priory in honour of St Faith was founded in this Norfolk village. Robert and Sybil Fitzwalter, wealthy Norfolk people, were captured by robbers on a visit to the south of France. They prayed to St Faith and were miraculously rescued. On their return to England, they vowed to build a priory in her honour. The wall painting includes a wheelbarrow, thought to be the earliest depiction of this Chinese invention anywhere in Western Europe.

If the connection between Conques and a Norfolk village is a surprise, it felt even more of a coincidence to have been to both within the space of ten days. I recalled some words of George MacLeod, the founder of the Iona Community. He led a retreat for students at Lancaster University during my under-graduate years there. It was typical of his generosity to give time to those very young in the faith. I scarcely appreciated his eminence then, but I remember one of his throwaway lines. Speaking of how our experi-ences can seem uncannily connected, he drew some examples from his own life and said, 'If you think that's a coincidence, I hope you have a dull life.'

George MacLeod was teaching about providence. The providence of God is a neglected theological subject. Perhaps we fear to speak of God's personal involvement with the world in case it leads to an assumption that God plans everything for us, depriv-ing us of our free will. But if we believe that God sustains the world by his love and provides for our wellbeing, time and circumstance are not indifferent to him nor is he indifferent to them. As we connect our experiences and interpret them in the light of God's loving care for us, we begin to see the inter-connectedness of all creation. We may find this in the most ordinary events, what the world calls coinci-dences, but in which we see something of the pattern of the divine interconnection between all things.

The interconnectedness of the Christian story over space and time made a forceful impression upon me on that day in Horsham St Faith. We were commemorating the life of a young Christian, about whom we know little, and who had been martyred 1,700 years previously. Local Christians in Agen facing persecution had acclaimed this young woman a saint and preserved her relics. Years later, the relics reached Conques, where they have been venerated by countless pilgrims. A couple from Norfolk in trouble in France credited their eventual escape to her intercession. Seventeen hundred years after her death, an Anglican congregation gave thanks for St Faith and for her Christian witness. People of very different levels of education, culture, language and spiritual sensibilities recognize that the Church as the body of Christ exists across space and time, creating a sense of unity that only a long perspective can give. The Pauline understanding of the members of Christ's body being united one with another is not related simply to a congregation at worship, nor to a particular Christian tradition, nor even to a single historical period. It is certainly not just related to those within the Church who are living now. I hear people refer sometimes to the Church 'dying out', but such a sentiment limits the Church to her members who are alive on earth today. It was Edmund Burke who described the State as a partnership between those who were dead, those who are living, and those who are yet to be born. That serves even better as a definition of the Church of

Jesus Christ. In Conques and Horsham St Faith I glimpsed that truth.

> *God of all creation, deepen our sense of the divine interconnection of all things, so that we may treasure our spiritual inheritance, take delight in present blessings, and trust what the future will bring because you are Lord of all. Amen.*

28

Lambeth Palace Chapel

Psalm 95.1–7

While Westminster Abbey and St Paul's Cathedral came through the Second World War relatively unscathed, Lambeth Palace was much less fortunate. A whole series of bombs destroyed much of the fabric. When the new archbishop, Geoffrey Fisher, arrived in 1945, a ten-year programme of restoration was put in place. The chapel, left a shell after the war, was restored only in 1955, and not entirely to everyone's satisfaction. When I joined the Lambeth staff in September 1987 and the chapel became the place for my daily prayers, I did not warm to it. Within months, however, we were worshipping in the crypt while the chapel above underwent bold and imaginative reordering.

The crypt had never been intended as a chapel at all, though it is the earliest part of the palace to survive, dating probably from around 1220. Archbishop Hubert Walter had decided it would be wise for him and all future archbishops to live rather nearer to the monarch than Canterbury, so created a home on the south bank of the Thames. In the light of what had happened to Thomas Becket not many years earlier, proximity seemed advisable.

The crypt was probably first used as a storehouse for wine and beer, and perhaps other foodstuffs too. In later years, it was often under water. The post-war reconstruction rendered it a place of storage once again, though much of what was stored there was soon forgotten. Cleared in 1987 and set up as a chapel for the first time, it seemed as if it was always designed to be a place of worship. Within weeks of the refurbishment, someone who joined the Lambeth community for Morning Prayer one day commented to me afterwards, 'You can tell this place has been sanctified by prayer for centuries.' I understood precisely why he said it, since I have scarcely known anywhere with a more unmistakeably 'prayed in' atmosphere. Somehow, also, it seemed appropriate to go below ground to undergird the archbishop and his ministry every day in prayer. Without prayer to support his work, no archbishop is going to survive for long.

The 1987/88 restoration of the chapel above took over a year. I didn't relish the thought of returning there for our daily worship. In the event, I grew to love it too, but for quite different reasons. While the Crypt Chapel seemed to convey its long history almost effortlessly, the main chapel's rebuilding and restoration in the mid-1950s had seemed rather sterile by comparison. The further restoration was an attempt to restore its memory and mystery. The screen separating the chapel and ante-chapel originally put in place by Archbishop Laud in the early seventeenth century was reintroduced. It had been restored following fire damage in the war but never put back in its original location. The stalls in the chapel were each allocated to a primate of the Anglican Communion, giving them a place at Lambeth Palace where so many bishops had been consecrated before being sent on mission overseas.

The boldest element of the restoration was the repainting of the vaulted ceiling. Leonard Rosoman was given the commission. Since he was already in his mid-seventies at the time, it was physically as well as artistically demanding. The ceiling is covered with images of the history of the archbishopric and Lambeth Palace's place within it. The vivid colours and the proportions of the figures cause many visitors to the chapel to respond initially with hesitation.

The scenes move chronologically from the west to the east end, concluding above the altar with a painting of the head of Christ in glory. At the west end, Augustine, the first archbishop, is depicted at the time he was sent by Pope Gregory the Great to England, the papal finger pointing in the direction in which a rather uncertain Augustine was to travel. The cruel hands of the knights killing Thomas Becket feature in the next panel. Then Thomas's rapid canonization is recalled as the boatmen on the Thames are seen doffing their caps in acknowledgement of Becket as they pass Lambeth Palace. Until the Reformation, Becket's image stood facing the river from the palace wall. The next vault portrays the consecration of Archbishop Matthew Parker, while, finally, a series of bishops are seen at their teaching desks at a Lambeth Conference, their hands raised in admonition and blessing.

The hands of all the figures are disproportionately large. Observers sometimes comment on this as if the artist got his perspectives wrong. Gradually the intention of the artist becomes clear. The history of this chapel, this archbishopric, the Christian faith itself, is an interaction between God and human beings in which the power of human hands is very significant.

Human hands can be creative or dangerous. Hands can destroy when holding a gun. The open hand can quickly become a clenched fist. It can be raised in frightening salute. Those old enough to remember the Second World War have never forgotten that. But hands can be tender as well. Hands calm the anxious child. Couples in love hold hands. In marriage, the joining of hands as vows are made provides a sacramental sign of commitment. Many of us use our hands every day to express ourselves.

Bishops use their hands as a sign of the gift of God's grace. They do so at baptism, confirmation, when celebrating the Eucharist, and in anointing the faithful. The hands seen on the ceiling of Lambeth Chapel are raised in blessing, defence, consecration, admonition and mission. They remind us of how much has been 'handed down' to us, and of our responsibility to hand this story on.

> *Lord Jesus Christ, you laid hands on the sick*
> *and took children in your arms. Ensure we*
> *use our hands creatively, so that the anxious*
> *may be calmed, the lonely comforted and*
> *all around us flourish through your loving*
> *benediction. Amen.*

29

Lakeland Motor Museum

2 Corinthians 4.5, 6

At Backbarrow, at the southern end of Lake Windermere, a motor museum of wide range and interest was established in 2010. The original collection of cars belonged to Donald Sidebottom and was formerly housed at Grange-over-Sands in the grounds of Holker Hall. But it outgrew those premises and now 30,000 motoring exhibits of one sort or another are on display. A separate exhibition on the same site is dedicated to Sir Malcolm Campbell and his son Donald's pursuit of land and sea speed records, which came to an untimely end with Donald's death on Coniston Water in 1967.

Malcolm and Donald Campbell were both household names in Britain. As a teenager I knew the current world land and water speed records. In those days that was not a sign of being a nerdy speed fanatic. There was a widespread general interest in such things, an interest that seems to have waned as the years have gone by. Perhaps it's because the vehicles used in record attempts now have such powerful jet engines that the skill of the driver seems more marginal. It cannot be because of a reduced fascination with speed itself. Motor racing remains popular and Formula One seems a licence to print money. However, our contemporary culture appears more focused on speed of communication, aided by the internet and the digital revolution more generally. Speed is now regarded as a virtue in itself. Rapid responses are more valued than slow, considered ones. There's very little in scripture or the Christian tradition to support such thinking. Jehu may have driven his chariot furiously (2 Kings 9.20) but he used it as a weapon in the death of Jezebel, and he is scarcely a good role model. In the New Testament, Christians are told to be 'slow to speak, slow to anger' (James 1.19).

The Campbell exhibition at Backbarrow prompts reflection on the quest for speed. It also tells a touching human story about the danger of 'driving furiously', whether on land, sea or metaphorically. But whom do we trust in life? Is it the person with the speediest reaction, or those quickest to make up their minds? Or do we value the wisdom of those who are slower to speak, and not easily vexed, whose long perspective is part of their maturity of mind? While nostalgia for an age of highly publicized record breaking may draw people to the Campbell exhibition, it leads to deeper questions too.

In the main Lakeland museum there are some iconic early automobiles and a range of veteran and vintage vehicles. But I found myself more fascinated by the commonplace cars of my earlier life that someone had taken the trouble to preserve. While it is always a pleasure to see an MGA or an E-type Jaguar, it was encountering the bubble cars I remember from my childhood that brought memories flooding back. There was even a Peel Trident, the smallest car ever manufactured in this country, built in the Isle of Man. An Amphicar was accompanied by a film of a happy family driving along a road and then straight into a river, upon which the car became a boat. It had such possibilities that you would have thought it would have been a commercial success. Perhaps most surprising was to see an Austin Allegro, one of the least cherished cars of all time, in mint condition. There was also an equally well-preserved Austin Metro. Two million Metros were built, and a caption accompanied the car with the line, 'When did you see the last one?' There are very few still registered. Yet, not long ago, they were being built in prodigious numbers.

At the Lakeland Motor Museum, these disregarded cars appeared to be transformed and given a new dignity. It seemed a reminder that what is commonplace and unheralded, and perhaps even despised, shines with a fresh and glorious lustre when it is loved. That's true for cars. It's true for human beings too. Those who are disregarded and unloved, failures and mistake makers, are still loved by God and made in his image. When you are used to seeing cars in a shabby condition, rusty and dishevelled, it is easy to forget that they once gleamed. The same is true for people.

I don't expect that everyone who was walking around the Lakeland Motor Museum with me had a theological experience, but our incapacity to see the lustre of the world in which we live was well illustrated there. There was beauty in these pristine and restored cars. Are we equally able to see the beauty in other people and just what the possibilities of human restoration may be?

The museum had some pictures and videos of the unveiling of new models and marques. Motor manufacturers love to build a sense of suspense and occasion. But the museum was also a reminder that what once seemed new, exciting and up to the minute gradually becomes duller over the course of time.

Classic car enthusiasts often expend vast amounts of time and labour and no little expense to give their vehicles renewed beauty. Sometimes we seem more willing to do that for a classic car than for one another. We tend to feel that those who have failed in life or become distressed, depressed or subject to mental illness, are rather lacking in lustre. But the people I know who shine most with the glory of God have often been those who have known suffering, or taken wrong turnings, and then been restored because someone has loved them and seen the glory in them.

When Moses was called to give the ancient people of Israel the divine commands by which they were to live, his face shone so much after he had been with God that he would dazzle them. So a veil was placed over him. There was only so much bright glory the people could take. Yet St Paul tells us there is no need for veils any more. God isn't hidden from us. We have seen his glory in the face of Jesus Christ. Seeing the glory of God in the face of Jesus Christ is as remarkable a thought now as it was two thousand years ago.

God, you reveal your glory in the face of Jesus Christ, enable us to see your beauty in our tarnished world and give us capacity to bring lustre to the lives of others through the grace of the same Christ our Lord. Amen.

30

Gammelstad, Lulea,
Sweden

Mark 10.6–9

The Diocese of Lulea is the northernmost diocese of the Church of Sweden, extending well into the Arctic Circle. It is twinned with the Diocese of Norwich. Clergy in Norwich look rather enviously upon their counterparts in Lulea, who have substantial paid staff teams even in rural areas, while Swedish clergy find themselves astonished to discover so much volunteer activity among the laity in England.

The city of Lulea, set on the coast of northern Sweden, grew up in the mid-seventeenth century. Nearby is Gammelstad, which is unlike anywhere else I have ever visited. It is a traditional church town of the sort found only in northern Scandinavia.

The scale, ambition and decoration of the late fifteenth-century parish church at Gammelstad suggest this was once a place of considerable prosperity. But, impressive though the church is, it is what surrounds it that makes Gammelstad a unique survival. Around 400 cottages make up the church town, many of them intended only for temporary use. They enabled families living far distant in the huge geographical parish to be religiously observant.

Sweden once had around 70 church towns, and there is evidence of at least ten in Finland. Royal decrees often required the population to be present in church on Sundays; even without compulsion, the desire to worship and hear sermons was greater in earlier centuries than now. And a longing for social interaction must have played its part in creating this tradition. The wooden cottages needed frequent repair, given the hostile winter environment, which makes the survival of so many dwellings in Gammelstad exceptional, and it is why it became a World Heritage site in 1996.

A traveller who visited Gammelstad in 1600 recorded how the farmers from miles around gathered in their cottages by the church during the Christmas season and often during ordinary weekends. The survival of so many buildings suggests the tradition lasted longer here than in many similar, but smaller, church towns. Evidence for social interaction among the young is provided by frequent condemnations by Swedish clergy of 'night-time courting'. Young men would often read poems outside the windows of young women, whose beauty they praised, begging to be let in to their houses. The watchful eyes of parents meant there was very little activity that was not chaperoned, but much matchmaking was done in this way.

My most recent visit to Gammelstad was on 13 June 2015, the day when Prince Carl Philip, the only son of the reigning King and Queen of Sweden, married Sofia Hellqvist at the Royal Chapel of Stockholm Palace. At Gammelstad that day (and, I believe, in a few other places in Sweden), the Church of Sweden offered 'walk-in marriages'. A couple could simply turn up at any time from 8.00 a.m. and a priest was on hand to conduct a marriage. There was an organist present, together with a couple of singers. The church even organized sparkling wine and wedding cake in the well-appointed church hall afterwards as a mini-reception. All the couple needed was what every couple intending to marry in Sweden requires, namely a marriage licence from the local tax office in the area. Ten couples married at Gammelstad that day, including one same-sex couple, since the marriage code in Sweden has been gender neutral since

May 2009. My wife and I attended a wedding of a Goth couple, both dressed in black, with about 20 guests.

One of the priests said that most of the couples would not have got married without this offer of hospitality from the church. It wasn't the church ceremony that put them off but the cost of everything that surrounds a wedding, since social expectations in Sweden are not much different to the rest of Western Europe. But in some cases, he added, circumstances and complexities in the couple's past relationships had inhibited them from approaching the church in the usual way. An unconditional welcome was important.

The hospitality offered by the church in Gammelstad that June Saturday was received gladly by people who clearly did not normally venture into church at all. The bridal couple at the wedding we attended were nervous, but their gratitude, especially at the reception afterwards, was evident. On a day when there was plenty of pageantry and grandeur on the streets of Stockholm because of the royal marriage, it was good to be part of a marriage ceremony that was no less important. I was reminded that within the Orthodox tradition, crowns are held above the bride and groom to express the conviction that in their union they are kings and queens of creation.

'You have crowned them with glory and honour, and set them over the work of your hands' (Hebrews 2.7, 8).

While there was something ennobling in the inspired move of the church in Gammelstad to do this for couples on the day of a royal marriage, at the same time the style and character of the wedding ceremony on offer prevented expectations of marriage being raised to a level that mere human beings cannot possibly fulfil. Marriage earths our relationships in the temporal character of human life, where our weaknesses and fallibilities are soon exposed. These couples seemed to have few illusions about themselves. Even so, the union of body and soul in marriage may make both partners more than they would each be individually.

The Scottish poet Edwin Muir attempted to capture this truth in his poem 'The Annunciation'. Reflecting on the way Mary surrenders herself to God's will that she should bear Jesus, Muir focuses on the unconditional character of the giving and the receiving in marriage that makes us more than we are. 'With my body I honour you, all that I am I give to you, and all that I have I share with you, within the love of God, Father, Son, and Holy

Spirit' is how the *Common Worship* marriage service expresses it. Marriage is, according to Edwin Muir:

> Where each asks from each
> What each most wants to give;
> And each awakes in each
> What else would never be.

Gammelstad is impressive as a reminder of the way a close-knit but dispersed community once formed around a parish church. In June 2015, it proved it was more than just a relic of history.

> *Take away our illusions about ourselves, Lord,*
> *as we give ourselves away to those we love as*
> *you have surely given yourself to us. Amen.*

31

Beeston Priory, Norfolk

Acts 4.32, 33

St Augustine of Hippo lived from 354 to 430.
The impact of his writings and ministry have
shaped the development of the Christian Church
ever since. Nearly 800 years after his death, a handful
of clergy seeking to live by a monastic rule written
by Augustine arrived in Beeston in north Norfolk.
A further 800 years later, the substantial ruins of
their priory were restored. Celebrations involved
hundreds of local people, many of whom probably
knew little about St Augustine. The restored ruins
gave them an insight into both life in their community centuries earlier and the influence upon it of a
bishop in North Africa long before that.

Augustine was Bishop of Hippo, now modern-day
Annaba in Algeria. In our own age, there are very
few Christians to be found there. Augustine died
in late August 430 when the Vandals were laying

siege to his city. His last recorded words were, 'see that the church library and all the books are carefully preserved for posterity'. Augustine believed in the power of the word, both the written word and the word of God. He knew that wars and conflicts destroyed civilizations and cultures, but thought that if philosophical and theological literature could be preserved, there was always hope for renewal.

We have more written material from Augustine than from any other ancient writer. From him we gain our understanding of the social, economic and cultural history of his time. There is one quotation of his that almost anyone who has ever heard of Augustine seems to know – 'Lord, make me chaste, but not yet.' In his early life he was a man almost overwhelmed with sexual desire, captive to his emotions, but he longed to live differently. He knew there was something or someone greater calling him. He eventually wrote a book called *Confessions*. Its title seems to promise a scandalous story. By modern standards, it may disappoint. But it was a new form of writing at the time. Augustine used his own personal story to illustrate much bigger themes: the power of good and evil and the destiny of human beings.

What Augustine explored in his literary works, he attempted to live out in community life too. In

Hippo, clergy and lay people lived around him in a form of the monastic life. In that setting he trained his clergy, and some of them went on to become bishops elsewhere. Prayer, worship and intellectual conversation were grounded in the routines of daily work. Augustine composed a Rule of Life. Some parts of it are addressed to women, although it is thought that the men and women did not live in one community but separately. Augustine could write at great length on almost any subject, but his Rule is very brief. It is also very practical and flexible. That's why it has survived over the centuries. It proved sufficiently appealing to be used by the founder of a small religious community in north Norfolk in 1216.

The Rule of St Augustine was little read and relatively unknown until the middle of the eleventh century. At that time, communities of clergy in northern Italy and southern France came together to live a common life of poverty, celibacy and obedience, in accordance with what they believed to be the example of the early Christians. Successive popes demanded that new religious orders should adopt existing Rules rather than create new ones, partly to bring some organization to what were becoming quasi-independent Christian societies, which potentially threatened good order in the Church, and the power of the papacy.

Some of these new groups looked to the Rule of
St Augustine because of its sanity and adaptability.
No pope could deny that it was an ancient rule. Yet
it was very flexible. Augustinian canons were thus
born centuries after Augustine himself had died.
In 1216 they reached Beeston, when Margery de
Cressy founded a priory dedicated to St Mary in
the Meadow. It was relatively unusual, since it was
an entirely independent priory answerable to no
larger religious house. There is a Norfolk motto –
'Do different' – and that seems to have been the
case here.

The scale of the present-day ruins is substantial, yet
Beeston rarely had more than four or five canons.
In their visitations in earlier centuries my predecessors as bishops of Norwich often discovered no
more than two canons living there. A few lay servants probably kept the place operative. The priory
was home to a small school for boys. Travellers were
given hospitality, especially pilgrims on their way to
the great shrine at Walsingham.

Even though there were few canons, some of them
knew how to get into spectacular trouble. In 1317,
one of them, John de Walsam, attacked the Bishop
of Norwich with a sword. Quite what the row was

about is unclear, but de Walsam was sent to Rome for the Pope to decide his future. Since the bishop recovered from the injury, the Pope absolved the erring canon and sent him back to the bishop to do public penance on his return. The bishop involved was John Salmon, who built a great hall beside the Bishop's Palace, in Norwich, the porch of which is still a ruin in the garden of the modern Bishop's House. It is a visible and daily reminder to the present bishop of the connectedness of Christian history.

In North Africa 1,700 years ago, St Augustine shaped the life of his community. In Norfolk 800 years later, a new community was founded based on his rule. This in turn was commemorated and celebrated by another bishop after another eight centuries had passed. Ancient Hippo, medieval Beeston and contemporary Norwich inhabit very different cultures with strikingly contrasting wealth, life expectancy and religious identity. Yet they have more in common than is immediately apparent. The thread between them isn't even Augustine, despite his brilliance of mind and largeness of heart. It is Jesus Christ, true God and true man, as Augustine believed and taught. The web of Christian history can catch us unawares. Ruins do sometimes speak.

*Open our hearts and minds, Lord, to the
wisdom, learning and holiness of scholars and
saints in centuries past, so that we may deepen
our sense of communion with those who have
believed in you in every age. Amen.*

32

Must Farm, Whittlesey

2 Peter 3.10–12

I began my ministry in 1975 on the outskirts of Peterborough. At first I found the flat fen landscape both forbidding and featureless. I soon learned that the dykes meant you had to concentrate hard when driving at night. In those years I used to visit a friend in Whittlesey fairly frequently and knew of the working quarry at Must Farm. On a foggy evening, it seemed as if the whole world could slip away and never be seen again. The atmosphere of the Fens on a wintry night was perfectly captured in Dorothy L. Sayers' *The Nine Tailors*. She knew from experience what it was to live in a fenland village.

A flat landscape is an open one. With good visibility you can see for miles. The skies are big. The spirit of fenland villages seems, though, to be one of very intense local loyalties, perhaps keener than in many other places. It is as if the openness of the landscape causes human beings to create enclosed communities to provide identity and locality. If so, this is no new phenomenon. A Bronze Age village built three thousand years ago was discovered at Must Farm in 1999 after an archaeologist noticed some wooden posts protruding from the edge of the quarry there. This led to a series of excavations, each one more extensive than the last, which gradually revealed the best-preserved Bronze Age settlement in Great Britain. A series of houses once built on stilts had sunk into the river below. The boundary of the settlement was defined by a palisade made up of large posts of ash, the wood coming from what seems to have been a well-managed plantation.

Pottery recovered from the site is of great range and quality. Storage vessels, elegant cups and clothing have been found. Textiles rarely survive but they did at Must Farm. Unexpectedly, much was made from plant fibres rather than animal hair or fur.

Most fascinating of all is the way in which the settlement seems to have come to a rapid end. It was subject to a fire that took hold so quickly that people seem to have fled at great speed. A bowl still contained the remains of a meal, including the spoon being used to eat it. The archaeologists working at Must Farm believe the settlement may have lasted only six months between its creation and destruction. Although the media called it Britain's Pompeii, it is on a very much smaller scale, and volcanic activity can probably be ruled out.

The circumstances of Must Farm's end may never be known. It seems as if the fire may even have been deliberate. Whatever the cause, everything slipped into the silt, which preserved it well. What's curious is that only a single human skull has been recovered. The resident community appear to have had just enough time to abandon the site. While the palisade suggests there was quite a bit to protect, it is possible the community may have destroyed its own buildings and fled. Perhaps they had word of armed marauders? We long to know more.

We can recover artefacts, skeletons and even houses. We know what our ancestors possessed. But it is harder to have any access to their character or the nature of their religious life. What made them sing for joy or weep with tears? What were the emotions of the people as they fled Must Farm?

The discovery that a place you once knew turns out to have great significance is a reminder of the significance of every place. Fresh information about places we already know often seems especially arresting.

Archaeological excavation uncovers layers of social, religious and cultural substance, too.

I vividly recall the Zeebrugge ferry disaster in 1987. Our family had travelled on that ferry line not long before. Such Channel crossings seemed routine and secure. The avoidable loss of life was tragic. But many stories of heroism emerged. One man used his body as a bridge to enable frailer people to move from an unsafe part of the ferry to one where there was a chance of survival. Four other men trapped on one of the lower decks took it in turns to hold the head of an elderly woman above the water. An eyewitness wrote later, 'Tragedy does not take away love; it increases it. Perhaps we are more loving people, more sensitive, more concerned for each other because of that moment of grief which overthrew our ideas of what things matter, and opened our eyes again to the importance of our common humanity.'

Such stories and reflections need to be remembered if future generations are to comprehend fully the consequences of any disaster or tragedy. The way human beings are willing to place themselves in greater danger for other people they do not know is illustrated time and again. Three thousand years on from the fire and desertion of Must Farm, such stories there are irrecoverable. But cherishing our common humanity isn't restricted to our own generation. Nor is the sort of desertion in the wake of devastation found at Must Farm confined to the Bronze Age. Hundreds, perhaps thousands, of people in our world are abandoning their homes every day in places of war and conflict. The story of Must Farm is unexpectedly contemporary, and desperate people are often courageous.

The most interesting thing about human beings is not what we own but who we are, and our surprising capacity when tested to be astonishingly unselfish. In the Christian tradition we call such things 'uncovenanted' mercies; grace operating in ordinary life. 'Thank God,' people say at such times, even if they may not believe in him. An uncovenanted mercy takes your breath away. It is a moment of revelation. I am sure that was as true three thousand years ago as it is now.

> *Give us the courage, Lord, to be unselfish*
> *when in danger, compassionate to those who*
> *have come through tragedies, and generous*
> *to migrants and refugees seeking a better*
> *life. Amen.*

33

The Holy House,
Shrine of Our Lady of Walsingham,
Norfolk

Philippians 2.1–3

North Norfolk seems an unlikely location for a Marian shrine, but apparitions of the Virgin Mary do not take much account of geography. My first visit to Walsingham was on a parish pilgrimage while I was still at university. The Shrine Church with its many altars and chapels confused me. I half expected the Holy House to bear a resemblance to a carpenter's workshop. The altar, the image and the countless candles in this windowless space made it seem claustrophobic. The religion was exotic and more High Church than anything I had ever experienced.

I truly connected with Walsingham once I was ordained and brought parishioners to the National Pilgrimage. When I saw what this did for those who lived and worshipped in a small church on a council estate, I knew its capacity to deepen the faith of simple believers and to simplify the faith of those blessed with learning. In 1980, when Robert Runcie became the first Archbishop of Canterbury to preside and preach at the National Pilgrimage, it felt as if the Anglican Shrine at Walsingham was now fully 'owned' by the Church of England. That experience, soon followed by the visit of Pope John Paul II to England, raised expectations that Anglican–Roman Catholic unity was just around the corner. We were mistaken, though at Walsingham, in spite of the fact there are separate Anglican and Roman Catholic shrines, relationships have never been better. Many Roman Catholic pilgrims now come to visit the Holy House in the Anglican shrine and to be sprinkled. It is the only Holy House in Walsingham, constructed in the 1930s but inspired by the same vision of the Virgin Mary granted to the Lady Richeldis as long ago as 1061 that led to the construction of an earlier Holy House destroyed at the Reformation. However, the laying of the foundation stone of the Anglican Shrine is a story in itself of contested Christian unity.

In 1921 the benefice of Walsingham with Houghton St Giles had been without a vicar for some time. Eventually a curate with a modest curriculum vitae – four brief curacies in succession – was appointed. His rather unusual name was Hope Patten. He came to Walsingham knowing it had been a pilgrimage centre until the Reformation. From the start, he sought the renewal of the tradition of pilgrimage, though how this would be achieved eluded him. Once he set up a renewed image of Our Lady of Walsingham in the parish church, a trickle of visitors were attracted. Early one morning, Bertram Pollock, Bishop of Norwich, was one of them. He was a low-church protestant and a vehement opponent of the revised Prayer Book. The Anglo-Catholics of the diocese did not look upon him with favour, but he lacked vigour in attempting to impose discipline upon them or anyone else.

The story of Bishop Pollock's visit to Walsingham in 1928 is well told in Colin Stephenson's book *Walsingham Way*. 'Do you teach your people to worship the Virgin Mary, Mr. Patten?' asked the bishop. 'Only in the sense that they worship their earthly mothers,' came the reply. The bishop instructed that all the new things that had been placed in the church should be taken away, whereby Hope Patten said he hoped to build a chapel to house the image on private property. Bishop Pollock remarked, 'That would be very kind', a statement of approval which he later regretted. When the foundation stone was laid for the Holy House of the new shrine, it was furnished with a Latin inscription dating the

193

event in the pontificate of Pius XI, Bertram being
Bishop of Norwich and Hope Patten parish priest of
Walsingham. The wording reached the press. Bishop
Pollock objected to the mention of the Pope. The
removal of the Pope's name was refused, so the
bishop asked to have his own name removed instead.
The foundation stone had already been carved,
which meant that Bishop Pollock's name had to be
filled in with plaster. This was later removed, so he
is mentioned after all, though he never once set foot
in the new shrine church established in his diocese.

Is that foundation stone a fiction or does it represent
a truth that we rarely consider concerning the place
of the Church of England in the one holy catholic
and apostolic church? It may be too easily dismissed
as an Anglican Papalist fantasy, just as Anglican
Papalism (if the majority of Anglicans have heard of
it all) is now largely disregarded and ignored.

Anglican Papalists believe that the Catholic Church
in England bifurcated at the Reformation. They
argue the Church divided into two branches, rather
like a two-pronged fork. So the true Church of
England, Anglican Papalists would argue, is not
merely the Church of England established by law,
but the Catholic Church in the land as a whole,
outwardly divided at present in the sense that the

Roman Catholic Church in England is not an intruded schismatic body but the other section of the pre-Reformation English Church. That is the thinking which inspired the foundation stone at Walsingham. It isn't a denial of our current separation, but expresses a belief that Roman Catholics and Anglicans do truly belong together within the one holy catholic and apostolic Church, even if its unity has not yet been realized.

Well before the re-establishment of the shrine at Walsingham, Anglican Papalists not only campaigned for the reunion of the Church of England with the Holy See but also prayed for Christian unity. Such initiatives in England caught the attention of a new religious community in the Episcopal Church in the United States at Graymoor in New York. As the twentieth century began, it was proposed that there should be an Octave of Prayer for Christian Unity, focused upon the reunion of the Anglican tradition with Rome. This ran from the Feast of St Peter's Chair in Rome (18 January) to the Feast of the Conversion of St Paul (25 January). It was promoted in Anglican Papalist circles on both sides of the Atlantic. Then, the religious community at Graymoor was received in its entirety into the Roman Catholic Church. It became known as the Franciscan Friars of the Atonement and continued to promote the Week of Prayer for Christian Unity. The week was commended by Pope Pius X as early as 1909. In 1916 Pope Benedict XV extended its observance to the whole Church. It continues to this very day on those dates. It embraces all traditions of Christians. Few of those who observe the week now realize it started life as an Anglican Papalist initiative.

Walsingham has taught me that when I declare my belief in 'one holy catholic and apostolic Church', it is not a theological theory or a pious aspiration. It is a living reality, damaged, broken, often ignored and sometimes despised, but earnestly prayed for. If we have learned anything about Christian unity in recent decades it is that it is unlikely to be negotiated as if it were a trade deal or diplomatic agreement. It will be received as a gift, for Jesus Christ wills his Church to live in unity.

> *Give us the vision, Lord, to recognize the*
> *diversity of our gifts and our unity in you,*
> *so that we may anticipate with joy the time*
> *when your whole Church is one in doing your*
> *will. Amen.*

34

Jorvik Viking Experience, York

John 1.43–50

About 30 years ago we took our young children to the Jorvik Viking Experience in York. Opened in 1984, it was a pioneering interactive exhibit, not to be confused with dull museums. Our children had something of an allergy to the very word 'museum', which usually prompted a cry of 'boring'.

The Jorvik Centre was not boring. You sat in a little car for a slow ride lasting about 12 minutes. It transported you back through scenes of York's Viking inheritance. The odours of the past were brought to your nostrils. They were not terribly appetizing, as I recall, but caused our children to giggle. There were dramatic if static scenes. The Viking Experience was brought to you, and you to the experience. Whether we or our children left any the wiser about the Vikings I rather doubt, but we undoubtedly had an experience.

The Jorvik Centre was flooded in 2015. It only reopened fully in April 2017. Intriguingly, there's rather more now in the exhibition about Christianity in the Viking age than there had been, and the Archbishop of York was invited to open it. I'm sure it's much improved. It is still popular. It is an 'experience'. Terry Eagleton has commented on our longing for 'experience'.

> It is sobering to reflect how many deprived souls in the past visited the Grand Canyon without knowing they were having a Grand Canyon experience. What we consume now is not objects or events, but our experience of them. Just as we never need to leave our cars, so we never need to leave our own skulls. The experience is already out there, as ready-made as a pizza ... and all we need to do is to receive it.

Timothy Radcliffe, the well-known Dominican, commented in one of his books that 'People no longer just shop. We want "the shopping experience". Airlines invite us to have a "flying experience" on our way to San Francisco where, on Fishermen's Wharf, we can have "The San Francisco experience".'

When we come to church, perhaps we expect the God experience to be packaged similarly. I expect we do, more than we often realize. It is how we have been conditioned. Experiences are delivered to us.

At York all those years ago we were passive receivers of the Jorvik Viking Experience. Not much was expected of us. We sat still in our cars. If we'd tried to get out and explore, we would have been swiftly ejected. Those who delivered the experience were definitely in charge.

Norwich Cathedral, like many others, sees thousands of worshippers on Christmas Eve and Christmas Day, and many more throughout Advent when, anticipating the feast, carol services take place almost daily. It would seem churlish to complain about such popularity. It's part of the 'Christmas experience' for many people. Regular worshipping Christians sometimes complain that they cannot 'join in' cathedral services. That's precisely why the services in question are so popular with many who do not go to church. An experience is given and gladly received. It is true that there are different ways of participation. I participate in classical concerts through my attention to the skills of musicians. But to become a worshipper there has to be a giving away of oneself, an offering, an expression of desire for God, usually supported and sustained by others. No one can worship for you.

We are not normally inclined to say, 'I have worshipped enough to last me for the rest of my life', even if some dire church services tempt us to think that way. The experience of worship ought to kindle ever greater curiosity about God.

Curiosity about the experience of following Jesus seems to have drawn the first disciples to him. Perhaps the most revealing encounter is between Philip and Nathanael in John's Gospel. When Philip tells Nathanael they have found the Messiah and that it is Jesus, son of Joseph, from Nazareth, Nathanael famously responds, 'Can anything good come out of Nazareth?' (John 1.46). Often interpreted as a reference to the low esteem in which Nazareth was held, it's more likely Nathanael was questioning the location, since Nazareth was never mentioned as somewhere to look for the coming Messiah. Philip simply responds, 'Come and see.' Come and meet Jesus. Come and experience an encounter with him and your life will be changed.

Jesus greets Nathanael with, 'Here is truly an Israelite in whom there is no deceit!' It's as flattering as Jesus gets. 'Where did you come to know me?' asks Nathanael. 'I saw you under the fig tree,' says Jesus. This prompts Nathanael to exclaim, 'Rabbi, you are the Son of God! You are the King of Israel!' (John 1.47–49)

None of this makes much sense at first sight. Why should Nathanael think that Jesus is the Son of God just because he has seen him under the fig tree? In the book of Susanna in the Apocrypha, remembering where you had seen someone was a sign of being a true witness. Nathanael recognizes Jesus as a true witness of God, who sees more than the surface of life, who stands in a great tradition but goes well beyond it. Jesus promises Nathanael that he will see greater things than this. There are many more experiences in store.

In his encounters, Jesus frequently causes people to believe he knows them better than they know themselves. Christians have always spoken of their experience of Christ as one that involves knowing and being known, opening a fresh way to God, triggering trust and love.

At their best, churches do this. The invitation 'Come and see' isn't for a brief pre-packaged experience that has no consequences for life. 'Come and see' isn't simply to observe the architecture, wonderful though that may be. It isn't even 'Come and see' the clergy or the bishop on an occasional visit, good though these things may also be. It is to come and meet Jesus, who knows you better than you know yourself. The experience on offer is of life in Christ. It's more than 'experience'. It is a foretaste of abundant life, life in all its fullness.

Welcoming God, as your Son invites us to share the life of your kingdom, may we call others to come and see Jesus, and so discover an experience of life in all its fullness. Amen.

35

Hellfire Corner,
Redruth Recreation Ground

Mark 11.7–11

My early experience of sermons was that they were often too long but, generally, much more about God's love than his wrath. An abundance of autobiographies and memoirs suggests that my early experience was unusual. Accounts of childhood adversely affected by the guilt and depression caused by hellfire preachers or the dark arts of priests and nuns are commonplace. The same tradition informs a great deal of fiction. James Joyce's novel *A Portrait of the Artist as a Young Man* was published in 1915. It includes a sermon by a Jesuit priest, who describes the nature of hell.

> Hell is a ... dark and foul-smelling prison,
> an abode of demons and lost souls ... the
> walls of which are said to be four thousand
> miles thick ... All the filth of the world,

all the offal and scum of the world, we are told, shall run there as to a vast reeking sewer when the terrible conflagration of the last day has purged the world.

This fictional sermon is preached to a congregation of schoolboys. I am glad things had changed by the 1950s.

My early perception of hell was formed less through attendance at church than from my familiarity with the Recreation Ground where Redruth play their rugby. To this day, one of the corners towards the try line slopes a little. The crowd, often a substantial one in my childhood, gathers there in close proximity to the pitch. The Cornish are not silent observers of rugby matches. The noise which greets visiting teams defending the try line in Hellfire Corner (as it is called) can be very intimidating indeed. Many of the teams that play at Redruth are not accustomed to being barracked by a crowd. The sense of being imprisoned and helpless, and certainly under fire, has made the Recreation Ground in Redruth feared by visiting teams. The reputation of Hellfire Corner adds to its deterrent value.

The passion of a crowd is powerful and can be frightening. The mood of a crowd can quickly change. The crowd that welcomes Jesus with cries of hosanna – 'Save us now' – as he enters Jerusalem quickly turn to shouting 'crucify him', days later.

Once, in my late teens, I was watching Redruth play the Welsh club, Tredegar. The match had developed into something of a brawl on the pitch, not helped by what the Redruth supporters considered atrocious decisions by a referee with poor eyesight. I was in the small grandstand and shouted out something uncomplimentary about the Welsh nation, whereupon a Welsh fist from the row in front made contact with my nose. Fighting on the pitch soon spread elsewhere. My elder brother intervened. It all calmed down reasonably quickly. Relationships were restored in the bar afterwards. But I have never forgotten it. It taught me how the passion of a crowd causes you to say or do things you never would if on your own.

On Palm Sunday, crowds greeted Jesus on his entry into Jerusalem. The reputation of this prophet from the countryside had gone ahead of him. He was a healer, a wordsmith, and a teacher of unusual power. He fed thousands. He made the lame walk and the blind see. No wonder they looked to Jesus with expectation. Jesus had gathered a following who had heard him speak about the coming of God's kingdom. For

205

those under the weight of Roman occupation, the expectations were political as well as religious.

Jesus did not please his public. He did not do what the crowd anticipated. Instead of confronting Pontius Pilate, the Roman governor, he made straight for the temple, the very heart of his own religion. He threw over the tables of the money changers. He showed no respect for the profit motive. He launched into a tirade against those who turned God's temple into a robbers' den. The money changers set up their stalls in the outer temple, the place reserved for Gentiles. Anyone could come there to approach God. That was its purpose. Jesus was not protesting primarily about the exchange rates that the moneychangers were offering. What appalled him was that they were excluding the very people for whom this was the place where they could meet the God of Israel. Taking away access to God was theft of the very worst kind. The money-changers robbed people not simply of currency but of access to the one God and Father of all.

This was not a message the crowd wanted to hear. So its mood changed. Within hours, Jesus had few supporters. Perhaps some in the crowd who had greeted him with cheers were those who now cried for him to be crucified.

We know all this to be true to our own experience. We know that someone who is celebrated one day in the media is knocked down the next. Popularity is transient. Crowds are fickle. So are we.

The terrifying reality of Holy Week is that it reveals the fickleness in us. We do want to love and serve God but we know our capacity to betray him. What we would really like is a comfortable religion, full of unchanging certainties. Jesus does not offer us that. He was – and is – a disturber of the people. He does not need to warn us about hell, though he does hold a mirror to our shortcomings.

Jesus was not long on comfort, but he was huge on compassion. He may not have pleased his public, but he still loved them. He may have been condemned to death by the crowd, but he still loved them. He may have been nailed to the cross by soldiers, but he still loved them. He may have been taunted by bystanders, but he still loved them. 'Father, forgive them, they know not what they do.' The same Jesus Christ knows our capacity to betray him. During Holy Week it is our fickleness, unfaithfulness and inability to live in love and peace that we bring to the Cross.

When the Passion narrative is read dramatically in English churches, it can be a very reserved shout of 'crucify him' which is heard. Perhaps we hope we would not have shouted for his death. My experience of crowds suggests otherwise. In any case, it is our sins and shortcomings, our petty betrayals and our big mistakes, that are the very reasons that Christ gave his life for us on the Cross of Calvary. By his wounds we are healed. That's why we continue to shout 'Hosanna', 'save us now'.

> *Compassionate God, give us such insight into our fickle loyalty to you that we recognize the need of your forgiveness, through the Passion and Death of your Son Jesus Christ. Amen.*

36

Dominus Flevit, Jerusalem

Luke 19.41–44

There is a magnificent panorama of the Old City of Jerusalem from Dominus Flevit, the modern church built on the Mount of Olives above the Kidron Valley. Completed only in 1955, the architect Antonio Barluzzi shaped this modest church to look like a teardrop. Luke's Gospel tells us that as Jesus 'came near and saw the city, he wept over it, saying, "If you, even you, had only recognized on this day the things that make for peace!"' (Luke 19.41, 42).

Luke tells us Jesus wept when he was approaching the 'path down from the Mount of Olives' (19.37). He would then have had an astonishing view of Jerusalem. The temple towered over the Kidron Valley below. Its vast marble columns and huge bronze doors would have gleamed in the sunlight. Herod's palace would have been clearly visible in its commanding position at the highest point of the city behind the Temple Mount. Jerusalem is believed to mean 'vision of peace', which may have prompted Jesus' reflection upon this city where there was no peace. 'The days will come upon you,' says Jesus, 'when your enemies will set up ramparts around you and surround you, and hem you in on every side. They will crush you to the ground, you and your children within you, and they will not leave within you one stone upon another; because you did not recognize the time of your visitation from God' (Luke 19.43, 44).

As so often, Jesus is taking familiar phrases from the Hebrew Bible (including the description of the siege of Jerusalem in Jeremiah 52) and applying them to his own time. Predictions of disaster for Jerusalem were common enough at a time when there were many zealot groups and nationalist insurgencies against Roman occupation. The words of Jesus may have then sounded conventional enough for a Jewish prophet of the period. The sacking of the city in AD 70 does not count as one of the great surprises of history. Jesus was not engaged in political prediction but promised a different kingdom, one that needed a deep change of heart. His entry to the city was a visitation from God. The visitor would be rejected. It is no surprise that Jesus wept.

The visitor who today sits in Dominus Flevit looking towards the Old City will notice the window is
etched with a chalice and paten, a reminder both of
Christ's sacrifice and of our remembrance of him.
The Temple Mount, where the Dome of the Rock
and the Al-Aqsa mosque are found, provides a visual
reminder that Jerusalem is not sacred simply to Jews
and Christians but to Muslims too. The divisions
of present-day Jerusalem make it hard not to weep.
Everywhere one looks there are towers, domes and
minarets – reminders that Jerusalem has been prayed
in and prayed over for many centuries. An Israeli
poet Yehuda Amichai wrote, 'The air over Jerusalem
is saturated with prayers ... like the air over cities
with heavy industry. It's hard to breathe.'

Perhaps no one has described the dense spiritual
atmosphere of Jerusalem better than Simon Sebag
Montefiore in his biography of Jerusalem. He writes,
'Jerusalem is the house of the one God, the capital
of two peoples, the temple of three religions and
she is the only city to exist twice – in heaven and on
earth; the peerless grace of the terrestrial is as nothing to the glories of the celestial.'

At Dominus Flevit the boundary between the terrestrial and the celestial is exemplified in the sheer
number of tombs and graves packed closely and as

211

near to the Temple Mount as possible. The dead await the Apocalypse, their earthly lives over but their heavenly lives awaiting the end time. Montefiore points out that many shrines, even many private houses, are built around tombs. With so many dead awaiting resurrection, Jerusalem carries its history heavily. The layers of past prayer and present hopes make it unique. Humankind's deepest longing for God finds focus here, and yet it is a history which is incomplete and where no single faith has exclusive possession. It is hard to breathe. Perhaps more tears have been shed over Jerusalem than over any other city on earth.

Jesus weeps over Jerusalem, but we also see him weeping when he reaches the deathbed of his friend Lazarus. Lazarus's sister Mary weeps too, along with 'the Jews who came with her also weeping'. In his Gospel, John records that Jesus 'was greatly disturbed in spirit and deeply moved ... [and] began to weep' (John 11.33, 35). Was Jesus simply moved by the grief of his friends? That's how it seemed at the time. 'See how he loved him!' we read. It's an understandable explanation. Why shouldn't Jesus weep? Yet some New Testament commentators say that the evangelist is keen to show that Jesus, rather than being distressed and disconcerted by the death of Lazarus, sees it as a chance to demonstrate the power and glory of God. His tears are of anger rather than loss. Everyone surrounding Lazarus professes a belief in the resurrection of the dead and yet they are weeping as if what has happened is so final that it is beyond the power of God to change. As Jesus raises Lazarus to life again, the tears change from sorrow to joy.

While it is true that we can be moved to tears by joy as well as grief, we may shed tears of anger, too. Tears carry powerful emotion and sometimes they change our perspective. Grieving people sometimes cry until they can cry no more. When Jesus weeps, whether over Jerusalem or at the grave of Lazarus, I am not sure we need to know precisely what sort of tears he cried or exactly what prompted them. There are many reasons to weep over Jerusalem, given its history and tragedies. Tears of love and tears of regret may seem much the same. Our resurrection hope as Christians does not prevent us crying when loved ones die. Those tears caused by the separation of death may also be accompanied by tears of hopeful anticipation of the gift of abundant life for our loved one.

In the book of Revelation there's a promise of a time when 'there shall be no more weeping'. That's when God will finally 'wipe away every tear from our eyes'

(Revelation 21.4). In the interim, there are many tears. The fact that Jesus wept is a grace to us as we watch and wait in present-day terrestrial Jerusalem, whenever we anticipate the celestial city, and when we shed tears of grief, lament or joy. The gift of tears is a means of grace.

> *Lord Jesus Christ, when sorrow overcomes us*
> *or anger inflames us, may the gift of tears*
> *drench us with the grace that comes from*
> *weeping as you have wept. Amen.*

37

The Sixth Floor, the Texas School Book Depository, Dallas

Luke 22.19-20

The Texas School Book Depository, constructed in 1901, is architecturally unremarkable. It has been a storehouse and offices, and from early 1963 it housed school textbooks and associated materials. From the sixth floor there is an excellent view of Dealey Plaza in western downtown Dallas. It was from there that one of the depository's employees, Lee Harvey Oswald, watched President Kennedy's cavalcade approach on the President's visit to Dallas on 22 November 1963. Oswald fired two, possibly three, shots to assassinate the President. Two days later, Oswald himself was shot dead by a local nightclub owner, Jack Ruby, who died of cancer before his own trial could take place.

President Kennedy's assassination was so shocking that, years later, people could remember exactly what they were doing when they heard the news.

I was just 12 at the time and was occupied with homework. That was unmemorable but I vividly recall my parents in tears. Since they had no American connection of any kind, it was a token of the impact John F. Kennedy had made on the world in his one thousand days in the White House. It was an era of optimism and economic progress, with a growing campaign for civil rights for the black population as well as concern about the increasing power of the Soviet Union. President Kennedy was not the sort of liberal who eschewed military confrontation.

Although Kennedy faced stiff political opposition, his charisma (and that of his wife Jacqueline) was immense. By modern standards he was astonishingly accessible to the public. Thousands of people thronged the streets on his visit to Dallas. He insisted on riding in an open car. Even though America had an unfortunate history of assassinating its presidents, it had not happened since 1901. Few predicted Kennedy would fall victim to such a tragedy.

I visited the sixth floor of the Book Depository in 1992, about three years after it opened as a museum commemorating what happened there a quarter of a century earlier. I went with some friends who lived in Dallas. They were curious to see it but, like me, a little apprehensive. Would it be a macabre experience? It turned out to be exceptionally restrained, informative and moving. I learned that day something about how to heal memories. A small and courageous group of Dallas citizens had resisted the repeated demands for demolition of a building that many local people hated as a symbol of a day of ignominy in their city's history.

Even if the building had been demolished, the memory of what happened would have been less easy to erase. During the years that followed the assassination, thousands came to Dealey Plaza each year in remembrance or curiosity.

Two local Dallas women, Lyndalyn Adams and Conover Hunt, resolved in 1979 to create the museum now found on the sixth floor of the Depository. Their persistence in the face of opposition required both spiritual and physical courage. Gradually they gained support from two local judges and some farsighted local philanthropists. The City of Dallas refused to issue a demolition order. Dallas County purchased the building. In time, it became the new centre of county government. This enabled the preservation of the sixth and seventh floors and the opening of the museum.

Communities experience corporate guilt, even if it is the actions of a single individual that cause a tragedy. 'We are a tormented town,' commented one of the civic leaders in Dallas after Kennedy's assassination. The global reaction was deep shock, and then grief. Cinemas closed. Entertainments were cancelled. Churches everywhere opened their doors for prayer. American embassies and consulates around the world were flooded with people offering condolences. This was intensified, since Dallas was a Republican city that had not voted for Kennedy in 1960 and in which his Civil Rights Bill faced intense opposition. On the morning before the presidential visit, a local newspaper in Dallas carried a full-page advertisement paid for by local businessmen protesting against Kennedy's policies. A month earlier, while in Dallas to give a speech on United Nations' Day, the UN ambassador, Adlai Stevenson, was spat upon and hit on the head with a placard. Yet 250,000 people turned out in the same city to greet the President's motorcade – a quarter of the whole population.

The Sixth Floor museum seems almost understated in its determination not to glamorize Lee Harvey Oswald, who receives relatively modest attention. What the museum does is to explain the context of the age, the mood of political life, the contrast between the President's worldwide popularity and some of the tensions in the United States itself which found their focus in Dallas. It then painstakingly takes the visitor through the events of the day with video footage, artefacts, displays and sound recordings. It uses eyewitness accounts and explains remarkably concisely the 25 years of investigations by the US government into the assassination. Finally, it looks at the legacy of President Kennedy. The author Walter Lippman once observed that 'The final test of a leader is that he leaves behind him other men of conviction and the will to carry on.' Lyndon B. Johnson's pledge, 'Let us continue', was a commitment to carry on Kennedy's work. No fewer than 50 bills already planned or suggested by Kennedy were taken through Congress by his successor.

I came to this museum with the curiosity of someone who remembered President Kennedy but without great emotional investment. Yet it was in the final room that I realized the spiritual and transformative power of this place. Some Americans, especially those from Dallas itself, had carried with them a cocktail of regret, guilt and remorse that this should have happened in their city. The visitors' book was full of appreciation. Many local people had needed courage to come, but found on the sixth floor a healing of memories they had barely expected. The dismembering of our emotions is one of the consequences of trauma. Remembering puts us back together, but we are no longer simply what we were before. The integration of context and event, past and present moment, are all part of it. No wonder Jesus left us with something to do to remember him. 'Do this in remembrance of me' is not trapped in past event but leads us to a new future. In Dallas I sensed afresh what true remembrance does when it does not shy away from horror and tragedy but acknowledges them and places them in a much larger context. On the Sixth Floor in Dallas, a place of dislocation and utter inhumanity was reclaimed. It had something of the Upper Room about it. That made it unforgettable.

> *God of mercy, take our regrets and remorse*
> *and refashion them into a true remembrance,*
> *so that we are given fresh hope in your*
> *redemptive love. Amen.*

38

Huer's Hut, Newquay

Mark 14.37–40

Set on Towan Head, high above Newquay's harbour, is the gleaming white Huer's hut. It was once both the home and work station for a huer, an experienced fisherman, who would watch for reddish-purple ripples on the surface of the sea. That was the giveaway for a large shoal of pilchards. The huer would cry, '*hevva, hevva*' (meaning 'they're here'), through a primitive megaphone, causing the fisher folk of Newquay to take immediately to their boats.

Half the town would respond to the huer's call, whatever they were doing. In 1833, when a funeral was taking place it was said that, once the cry went up, only the vicar, the sexton and the deceased's body remained in church.

Men, women and children each had a designated role. The huer would direct the movement of the boats using a local form of semaphore, the signals being made by furze bushes covered with cloth. It was a responsible post for an experienced pilchard fisherman. The essential skills included an ability to keep watch for long periods as well as rapid reactions and a strong voice.

The Huer's hut was less than half a mile from where I lived in Newquay as a child. From its deserted yet prominent site, the view of the harbour and the bay remains the best in the area. It was a building which captured a child's imagination. I recall the Huer's hut featuring prominently in a story I wrote at my primary school during the weekly lesson then called 'composition'. It was both a commanding place, almost like a lighthouse, and yet it seemed what it surely was – a leftover from a previous era. Once vital to the life of the town, the Huer's hut had become a rather neglected monument. More recently it has been restored, and it is now gleaming white again and a Grade II listed building.

It's thought to date from as long ago as the fourteenth century, well before Newquay came into being as a fishing village. In origin, it could have been a hermitage. It was on the edge of the world, a demanding place in which to live, and open to the elements. Asceticism was imposed. That was the point. While the hermit would not have been there to watch for shoals of fish, the panorama provided a constant reminder of the power of him 'who moved over the face of the waters' (Genesis 1.2; adapted from RSV).

There are two regular occasions when the image of the Huer's hut springs to my mind. The first is at the ordination of priests, when those to be ordained are told they are to be 'messengers, watchmen and stewards of the Lord'. That phrase remains part of the bishop's charge to the candidates, as it has been for centuries. It has escaped the liturgical revisers, not least perhaps because of its biblical credentials. Now that night-watchmen with their braziers are almost as scarce as huers, it may seem that to be a 'watchman' is archaic and, even, too gender-specific. But the sense of being constantly alert to the coming of the Lord is an essential characteristic of the Christian life, of which the priest is to be a reminder to the faithful. 'I have posted watchmen on your walls, Jerusalem, who shall not keep silence day or night. You who invoke the Lord's name take no rest ...' (Isaiah 62.6, 7).

In the Passion story, when Jesus and his disciples reach Gethsemane after their meal in the upper room, it is late. The disciples are tired and sleepy.

223

Jesus asks them, 'Will you not watch with me one hour?' (Mark 14.37) The watching is important. 'Keep awake and pray that you may not come to the time of trial' (Mark 14.38). Jesus is gentle with the disciples' inability to keep awake. But he recognizes that their failure to be alert means they will fall into temptation when faced by a crisis or moment of truth. And so they do. They deny Jesus and run away. Our weakness overcomes our best intentions and prevents us doing what we know we should. That's why we are called to watch over each other in the Christian Church. One of the most powerful liturgical moments in the year is when the altar is stripped bare on Maundy Thursday, and we leave church in silence, remembering that the disciples forsook Jesus and fled.

The huer and his hut comes also to my mind whenever I read John 21. The risen Lord gives instructions to the disciples about where they should place their net. If they cast their net on the right side of the boat, they will find some fish. They do 'and they were not able to haul it in because there were so many fish' (John 21.6). Simon Peter jumps into the lake and eventually he and his friends haul in the net overflowing with fish. Even the number of the fish is recorded: 153. One hardly imagines they sat and counted them. There has been plenty of debate about what this number means. It is symbolic in some way. The total of the numbers 1 + 2 + 3 up to 17 makes 153. The numbers 10 + 7 (making 17) were once thought to signify a perfect whole. Others have claimed that 153 was the known number of species of fish in first-century Palestine. We don't know what was in the mind of the gospel writer in recording the number. What we do know is that he wanted to impress upon us just how amazingly prodigious the catch of fish under the direction of Jesus turned out to be. Jesus goes in for super-abundance. When he feeds the five thousand there is a huge amount left over. In his first miracle at Cana, there are gallons of the finest wine, more than anyone needed. When answering the call and instruction of Jesus, and doing his will, the disciples, these 'fishers of people', draw in a catch beyond their wildest expectations. So it shall be when the Church is obedient to the call of Jesus the huer.

Call us, Lord, to launch out in your service, confident in your guidance; and when we fail or fall asleep, may we hear your gentle voice of correction and respond afresh with wonder at your patience. Amen.

39

The crypt, Canterbury Cathedral

Romans 8.10, 11

The crypt of Canterbury Cathedral is built on a scale almost unmatched for size and beauty. In itself it is a substantial Romanesque church, partly but not entirely below ground level. Its high-level windows mean that even on a cloudy day it is much lighter than its name suggests. The crypt is not an inert foundation but a living heart for the cathedral above.

Dating from the time of Prior Ernulf, it was constructed from 1096. An array of mythical beasts adorn the capitals of a long series of arches. They seem bereft of religious significance (perhaps it was the stonemasons' doodling?). At the eastern end, two transepts contain chapels, one now housing the Huguenot congregation that has worshipped at Canterbury for well over a century. There's something apposite about Huguenots who once fled persecution coming to Kent and their successors worshipping partially underground.

The eastern end of the crypt was rebuilt and extended from around 1180, initially to provide a better and more dignified (and accessible) place for the mortal remains of Thomas Becket. As his cult developed and pilgrims came in ever greater numbers, something had to be done. Eventually the Trinity Chapel and the Choir above would become the permanent home for Becket's shrine. The crypt would return to being a place filled with altars in its various chapels for the monks to say their private masses each day. Even in our generation, it is not short of altars.

So the crypt continues to be a place of prayer. I have prayed there during quiet days and retreats, attended the Eucharist and even presided at a marriage. But I have also spent a great deal of time waiting around there, prior to the consecration of bishops or before Opening or Closing services at successive Lambeth Conferences. The crypt sometimes becomes a massive robing room. Below the great cathedral, those about to become bishops make their declarations and swear oaths. It's the place where bishops from all over the world gather in their hundreds in the cradle of Anglican Christianity. Sometimes they are moved to tears by the experience, especially if they have rarely travelled from their homes in remote parts of Africa or Asia. The cultural, racial and linguistic diversity of the Anglican Communion becomes visible on these occasions. Bishops of all shapes and sizes (and as the years have gone by, both male and female bishops too) struggle to get into their cassocks, rochets and chimeres (Anglicans have exotic terms for robes). Once they do so, they begin to look increasingly similar. The racial differences of the faces are not hidden, but when the bishops are robed, their matching dress becomes a vivid symbol of unity in diversity.

Early in 2011, a new sculpture was introduced to the crypt. Suspended above the place where Thomas Becket's grave was once situated, Antony Gormley's *Transport* is cast in the shape of a human body. It is made entirely of antique nails recovered after the repair of one of the roofs of the cathedral. *Transport* is a great deal more than a lesson in recycling. Nails have their own resonances for Christians, but the sculpture is primarily a study of the human form. Antony Gormley said:

> The body is less a thing than a place; a
> location where things happen. Thought,
> feeling, memory and anticipation filter
> through it sometimes staying but mostly

passing on, like us in this great cathedral
with its centuries of building, adaptation,
extension and all the thoughts, feelings
and prayers that people have had and
transmitted here. We are all the temporary
inhabitants of a body. It is our house,
instrument and medium; through it all
impressions of the world come and from
it all our acts, thoughts and feelings are
communicated.

The sculpture floats above worshippers, pilgrims
and tourists as well as robing clergy and bishops.
The nails give it real substance while, at the same
time, the body is transparent – fragile as well as
solid. You gaze through it. It becomes a reminder
that our bodies are vacated at death. The capacity of
the sculptor to create a sense of both substance and
slightness means that *Transport* is capable of many
interpretations.

When I first saw this sculpture I was surprised that it
seemed smaller than I expected. Then I discovered
it is based on the proportions of Antony Gormley's
own body, a reminder of how small even a tall man
can seem compared with the dimensions of a great
cathedral. The body is both visibly present and yet
strangely uninhabited.

Many of us seem to dislike our bodies. Perhaps it is the consequence of glamorous images of celebrities. There is certainly a very large industry dependent on those of us who think we are too fat, too wrinkled or too thin. The cosmetics industry makes billions as we fight the ageing process. A television series called *Embarrassing Bodies* suggests that some of us are even fascinated by people more misshapen than ourselves.

Following his martyrdom, it was discovered that under his clothes Becket wore a hair shirt, one that stretched to his knees. Goat's hair continuously chafing the skin would make anyone miserable. At the time, the fact that he led such a life of self-mortification was taken as a further sign of Becket's sanctity. In the early Middle Ages this was the accepted way of taming the physical cravings of the body, which was regarded as the supreme location of carnal desires. In Becket's day, the body was regarded as a snare and a trap. It's odd that such negative thinking became so common in Christianity, given that St Paul used the body as a powerful image of the beauty and unity of the Church. Think, for example, of the way he speaks of the way Christ transforms 'our lowly body to be like his glorious body, by the power that enables him even to subject all things to himself' (Philippians 3.21).

In the crypt of Canterbury Cathedral Antony
Gormley has made a body of fragile beauty out of
discarded scraps. To have done this in one of the
sacred places of the mother church of the Anglican
Communion is a vivid reminder of the value of our
bodily humanity. For those who wait in that place
for some of Anglicanism's biggest services, it's a
meditation too on the glory of the body of Christ.

*Incarnate Lord, as we treasure the image of
the Church as your body, we rejoice that you
took flesh and gave our human bodies a new
dignity as places of your habitation. Amen.*

40

The Lost Gardens of Heligan, Cornwall

Ezekiel 36.33–36

More than five million visitors have explored the Lost Gardens of Heligan near Mevagissey since their restoration in 1992. Two hundred acres are now open to the public. The Tremayne family bought the estate in the sixteenth century. The gardens were developed largely in the nineteenth century, including an area filled with tree ferns called 'the jungle', alongside curiosities such as the only pineapple pit remaining in Europe, the heat provided by rotting manure.

The restoration of Heligan was the subject of a six-part documentary on Channel 4 twenty years ago. It has since revitalized the local economy. None of it would have happened without the imagination and determination of Tim Smit, who saw what lay beneath the accumulation of decades of undergrowth. He went on to create the nearby Eden Project.

The story of Heligan is typical of many of the great houses of Edwardian England. The First World War claimed many men who worked on the land, gardeners included. Heligan had 22 gardeners before 1914 and there is a moving photograph of them just before the war broke out. The wider social changes brought about by the war led to many great estates being sold and country houses abandoned. What made Heligan different was that its owner, Jack Tremayne, moved to Italy in the 1920s and allowed the house to be tenanted. In succeeding decades the garden simply disappeared as nature took over. Not all was lost, for some of the colossal rhododendrons and camellias to be found now at Heligan enjoyed unrestrained growth for many years. These plants come from a past horticultural age, some of them raised from seed collected by the celebrated plant hunter Joseph Hooker in India during an expedition between 1847 and 1851.

Early visitors to Heligan returned time and again to see the progress made in its restoration. Its beauty, variety and colour at almost any time of year owes much to its sub-tropical setting, but there is also romance in the story. The forces of nature would

overtake the gardens once more if the present substantial workforce disappeared. The gardener works
with nature but battles against nature too.

The Bible has a high doctrine of gardens. It is no
surprise that Tim Smit gave the name Eden Project
to his second huge enterprise. The book of Genesis
opens with a vision of paradise in which 'the Lord
God planted a garden in Eden' (Genesis 2.8).
This garden is laid out by God, who carefully creates plants, animals, birds and fish, all of whom live
together according to God's will. Then God creates
man, puts him in the garden and gives him a woman
as his companion.

The garden suffers no natural disaster. It is the man
and woman who disturb its equilibrium. To be
more accurate, the man blames the woman, and the
woman blames the snake in the grass. In the story
of the Fall we read of the terrible consequences of
human sin – a world of suffering, hard labour and
exile. As stories go, the biblical narrative of the Fall
is one of the most vivid ever told.

A visit to Heligan prompts me to think more about
the biblical Garden of Eden than does the Eden
Project. For the prophets teach that the restoration
of the garden in Eden is the final purpose of history.

Through Ezekiel God says that on the day when he will cleanse his people from all their sins, the waste places will be rebuilt and 'the land that was desolate shall be tilled ... and become like the Garden of Eden' (Ezekiel 36.34, 35). Amos, Isaiah and Joel share the same vision. God wants to bring his people and his creation back into perfect unity. The struggle isn't with the sun, the sky, the sea and the stars. They seem to be remarkably reliable. It is human beings who need to return to God's ways. In creating a garden, and perhaps even more in restoring one, human beings work in harmony with God's good purposes in creation.

What is it about gardens which appeals to us so much? Is it the way in which living things, plants and flowers, are so arranged that we experience order in creation? Is a garden a symbol of our world as it is called to be? For a garden only exists at all because human beings work with the creativity of nature to bring about peace, order, beauty and harmony. Perhaps our gardens are bigger homes of theological truth that we sometimes think. The clergy don't much care for Dorothy Frances Gurney's poem that declares, 'one is nearer God's heart in a garden than anywhere else on earth'. It has been used too often in England as an excuse for not going to church. But perhaps she was a better theologian than we think.

There is very little about the natural creation in the New Testament. Even so, gardens are important. They are the setting for the most important events. It is to a garden – Gethsemane – that Jesus leads his disciples after the Last Supper. This is one of the easiest sites in Jerusalem to identify, lying as it does between the city and the Mount of Olives across the Kidron River. The betrayal of Jesus takes place not only in a garden but with a kiss. It is a sign of love going wrong. The link with the story of the Garden of Eden could not be plainer.

But it does not finish there. In John's Gospel Mary Magdalene mistakes the risen Christ for a gardener. Christ's resurrection is discovered in a garden at the break of day.

The story of the Fall in the Garden of Eden explains how, theologically, our disordered world is also God's good gift in creation. In the resurrection garden we see that disorder does not have the final word. St Paul describes Christ's resurrection as 'first fruits'. Put another way, Christ's resurrection is the sign of the imminent resurrection of others, just as the first handful of ripe grain is a sign of a harvest that must very soon be gathered.

Every gardener knows that keeping an earthly garden is hard work. Those who have laboured at

Heligan over the years know that restoring one is even harder. And it is never complete. We know that our human efforts will never restore paradise. That's why in the garden of the resurrection our new life in Christ comes entirely as gift.

> *Risen Lord, you gave new life in the Easter garden to those who trust in you. Help us rebuild the waste places of the earth, that the whole creation may sing your praise; and through the Easter hope give us the vision to anticipate the coming of your kingdom on earth as it is in heaven. Amen.*

EASTER COLLECT

Eternal God,
whose Son Jesus Christ is the way, the truth, and the life:
grant us to walk in his way,
to rejoice in his truth,
and to share his risen life;
who is alive and reigns, now and for ever. Amen.

ACKNOWLEDGEMENTS

Caroline Chartres at Bloomsbury has been a source of wise encouragement and support as this book was written. I am grateful also to Nick Fawcett for many helpful comments on the script and to Jamie Birkett for guiding the book to publication.

My PA, Coralie Nichols, has been a tower of strength at every stage. Alison Hovesen and Marie Kuczak, also part of the secretarial team at Bishop's House in Norwich, have patiently typed many chapters alongside their duties.

Many of the places described in this book have been visited in the company of my wife, Julie. Her constant support and understanding makes it possible to reflect on shared experiences and much else besides.

PERMISSIONS